D1028482

THE CORE OF
Johnny Appleseed

The Core of Johnny Appleseed

The Unknown Story of a Spiritual Trailblazer

RAY SILVERMAN

Illustrations by Nancy Poes

SWEDENBORG FOUNDATION PRESS
West Chester, Pennsylvania

Library of Congress Cataloging-in-Publication Data

Silverman, Ray.

The core of Johnny Appleseed : the unknown story of a spiritual trailblazer / Ray Silverman ; illustrated by Nancy Poes.

p. cm.

ISBN 978-0-87785-345-9 (alk. paper)

1. Appleseed, Johnny, 1774-1845. 2. Nursery growers—United States— Biography. 3. Businessmen—United States—Biography. 4. Conservation- ists—United States—Biography. 5. Tree farmers—United States—Biography. 6. Apples—United States—History—19th century. 7. Appleseed, Johnny, 1774-1845—Religion. 8. Spiritual biography—United States. 9. Swedenborg, Emanuel, 1688-1772—Influence. I. Title.

SB63.C46S55 2012

634'.11092—dc23

[B]

2012016861

Edited by Morgan Beard
Design and typesetting by Karen Connor
Index by Laura Shelley

Printed in the United States of America

Swedenborg Foundation Press
320 North Church Street
West Chester, PA 19380
www.swedenborg.com

This book is dedicated to all those who have endeavored to faithfully preserve and pass on the timeless story of Johnny Appleseed. You have sown, and others have reaped. As Joe Besecker, director of the Johnny Appleseed Museum, likes to say, "May apple blessings be yours, forever."

I saw gray Johnny Appleseed at prayer . . .
Praying, and reading the books of Swedenborg
On the mountain top called "Going-To-The-Sun."

—Vachel Lindsay (1879–1931)

Contents

Foreword

I grew up in Orange County in southern California. When I was a youngster in the 1950s and '60s, there were actually orange groves there. Of course, being southern California, there were also palm trees, beaches, deserts, and the beginnings of urban sprawl.

Some would say I lived in the promised land, the golden end of the westward trail. But my heart and imagination were some three thousand miles away in the dense forests, fertile valleys, and westbound rivers where the pioneer trails began.

I have always loved American folklore, or "tall tales," as they're sometimes called. My first exposure to these stories was probably from watching *The Wonderful World of Disney* on Sunday nights. Through Disney's famous animation, I came to know the likes of Paul Bunyan, Pecos Bill, and my favorite, Johnny Appleseed.

Unlike Paul Bunyan or Pecos Bill, Johnny was a real person. His name was John Chapman, and he came into this world about the same time as our country. He couldn't chop down entire forests or lasso a river, but he became a legend to the pioneers because of his love for others and his service to the land and its people. Now that's an amazing feat.

As you can imagine, when a man has been gone from the world for over 160 years the facts and fictions of his life can get mixed together as people tell and retell the stories about him. On top of that, it seems that Johnny enjoyed the tales about himself and liked to polish them up bright and shiny, like his apples.

Fortunately for us, Dr. Ray Silverman has delved into the mountain of material available about Johnny. (Take a look at his acknowledgements and endnotes!) Like me, Ray has a deep affection for Johnny Appleseed. That, combined with his skill as a researcher and his thoughtful approach, enables him to present us with a fresh view of both the man, John Chapman, and the legend, Johnny Appleseed. What he shows us is both surprising and—for people whose view of this American icon has been distorted by recent media portrayals—encouraging.

Ray generously provides many of the old "tall tales" about Johnny, and that is as it should be. After all, it is through these stories that we have come to know the man. As Ray writes: "While many of the stories are exaggerated and some are improbable, there is a core of truth within them that tells us a great deal about Johnny Appleseed." As a result, we have a picture not of a diminutive or meek fellow, but of a hardy man whose legend grew as our country did.

It's been many years since the first stories about Johnny began to spread through frontier towns, and they are still told and retold today. For example, here's something you might hear around a campfire on an Indiana summer night:

Freedom and the open road were Johnny Appleseed's birth-rights, and did he ever use them! There weren't any asphalt highways, not even a Motel 6 back then, my friend. He mostly walked, and barefoot at that. It was said he could melt ice with the soles of his feet! It's true that Johnny had an easy-going spirit, but that's understating it by a mile. He could doze whether he was hiding from Indian warriors or just floating down a river in a hollowed-out log. Of course, he loved animals and they loved him right back. Why, I have heard it said that Johnny freed an old wolf from a trap, and danged if that beast didn't follow him around like a little puppy! And do you have any notion of how many apple trees he planted across this country? Put another log on that fire, my friend. The night is young.

That's the short version.

Now, people might wonder, "How did John Chapman come to be Johnny Appleseed? What made him the way he was?" These types of questions, however, are never easy or simple. Any attempt to answer them would have to include Johnny's faith, and this is exactly where Ray shines a fresh light for us.

Johnny Appleseed was a Christian, originally a Congrega-tionalist. However, in the course of his travels he was intro-duced to the teachings of Emanuel Swedenborg and became a Swedenborgian, a member of the New Church. Ray is also a Swedenborgian and a professor of New Church theology. In *The Core of Johnny Appleseed* he brings his knowledge of Swedenborg's teachings to bear on Johnny's life and rewards us with a new perspective many biographers of John Chapman have missed.

I could go on, but I think it's time to let Ray introduce you to one of America's most beloved figures. I am referring, of course, to Johnny Appleseed, a pioneer and an adventurer who wandered unhindered through our newborn country. He was an entrepreneur and a smart businessman who used his vision and foresight to spread apple orchards wherever new settlers could use them. Most importantly, he was a man of faith who actually lived what he believed and became one of his church's greatest missionaries. He was the true prototypical American, and he should serve as an example for us and for future generations.

If you've never met Johnny Appleseed, prepare to be impressed. If you think you know him already, prepare to be surprised.

Thank you, Ray!

—*Rob Rumfelt*
www.theoldbookjunkie.com

THE CORE OF
Johnny Appleseed

1 ∽
The Open Road

Afoot and light-hearted, I take to the open road . . .

—Walt Whitman

The Early Settlers

When the European settlers arrived on America's eastern shore, they must have marveled at the opportunities that lay before them. America was vast, beautiful, and teeming with rich resources. It was not, however, an uninhabited land; nor was it "virgin territory." Indigenous tribes were spread throughout the land, each with its unique language, customs, and spiritual practices. The mountain ranges, valleys, meadows, rivers, and plains had long been home for the native people. The forests were thick, but there were also many trails to follow, some blazed by deer, others by the native people.

The story of the relationship between the original inhabitants of North America and the early European settlers is far from simple. Mistakenly called "Indians" by Christopher Columbus (who thought he had traveled to India), the native people did not always receive the outsiders with open arms. The early histories, written from the viewpoint of the European settlers, told frightening tales of "Indian" brutality, midnight raids, and horrendous tortures inflicted upon the apparently innocent settlers.

From the viewpoint of the American Indians, however, the settlers were far from innocent. In some cases, the settlers were indeed welcomed, and the gifts they exchanged were highly valued. Over time, though, misunderstandings arose, promises were broken, and hostilities ensued. Generally speaking, the settlers came to be seen as hostile trespassers who did not acknowledge the American Indians' ownership of the land or their way of life.[1]

Because of the complexity of these initial encounters, it is sometimes difficult to place the blame on either side. But it is reasonable to conclude that misunderstanding, greed, and selfishness were, as always, contributing factors.

These were not easy times for the early settlers. In addition to potential conflicts with tribes who resisted their intrusion, they had to deal with hunger, malnutrition, disease, and countless other hardships of wilderness survival. And yet, even though there were many opportunities for discouragement, the settlers remained inspired by the rich possibilities that lay before them. America was still a veritable "promised land" of fresh, new opportunities and thrilling prospects. This included not only the thirteen colonies established along the Atlantic coastline between 1607 and 1732, but also the beautiful mountain ranges and fertile valleys that beckoned from the west. Narrow wilderness trails were becoming open roads as rumbling wagon wheels widened them daily. It didn't take long for the Atlantic coast settlers to respond to the exciting words, "Go west, young man."

The Wild Frontier

The words "Go west" may have touched a place in the settlers that was different from the original call that had brought them to the New World. While many came in search of religious liberty and political freedom, they would now head west in search of fortune and adventure. They went forth to find places to raise families, start farms, form communities, and establish businesses. The dream of religious and political freedom was still alive; but a new dream was emerging as well—a dream of economic security through land acquisition and business development. A poor tenant farmer from Europe could now become a rich and independent land owner in America.

Beginning first with just pack animals walking along narrow trails, they later traveled in covered wagons, ever broadening the westward path. Among those who headed west were the rugged individualists who hitched up their wagons, climbed aboard with their families and possessions, and ventured forth to forge new frontiers beyond the Allegheny Mountains, some traveling as far as California. The settlers had come to believe that their government, after many wars and peace treaties, now owned the land, and through working hard they too could own a share of it. Prosperity was just around the corner, or rather, just beyond the next mountain range.[2]

American history is filled with stories about the legendary heroes of those days. It is said that Daniel Boone (1734–1820), a famous hunter and soldier, was captured five times by the Shawnee, but managed to escape every time. When he was not fighting against or escaping from American Indians, he was trapping beaver, hunting deer, and blazing (or at least widening) the "Cumberland Gap," a trail through the Appalachian Mountains called the "great gateway to the West."[3]

Davy Crockett (1786–1836), "the great bear hunter," was known as a fearless soldier who served as a mounted rifleman.

He eventually died while defending the Alamo Mission in Texas against a Mexican invasion. Only two Americans survived the battle. Ever afterward, the words "Remember the Alamo" became a battle cry to avenge the loss of American soldiers like Davy Crockett.

Then there was "Wild Bill" Hickok (1837–1876), the rugged lawman of the Old West who is said to have killed over one hundred outlaws in his lifetime. According to some accounts, he always wore two pistols, even while sleeping, and was lightning fast on the draw. He also loved to gamble, but met his demise when he was gunned down in a deadly poker game.

This list would not be complete without mentioning "Buffalo Bill" Cody (1846–1917), the famous scout, who earned his name by hunting and killing over four thousand buffalo in less than eighteen months. He later went on to preserve the memory of frontier days through "Buffalo Bill's Wild West," a circus-like show that featured live enactments of stagecoach robberies, raids on wagon trains, and fully costumed reenactments of famous battles such as Custer's Last Stand and the Battle of Little Big Horn. One of the most famous participants was the Sioux leader Sitting Bull himself.[4]

A Different Kind of Hero

Amid the rough-and-tumble background of the Wild West, with its deadly duels, animal slaughters, barroom brawls, attacks on pioneer settlements, and raids on American Indian villages, there arose another hero. His name was John Chapman (1774–1845).

Instead of a rifle, he carried a bag of seeds; instead of killing animals, he lived cooperatively with them; instead of fighting American Indians, he befriended them. In many ways, he was a cultural genius, a friend to European settlers and American Indians alike, a welcome guest in every home, loved by children, respected by their parents, and esteemed as a medicine man by the indigenous people.

Over time he became known affectionately as "Johnny Appleseed," the gentle hero of the pioneer times. His story was told and retold, with many changes along the way, and eventually became one of the most beloved stories of the American frontier.[5]

The most famous telling of Johnny's story is the 1948 Disney classic *Melody Time.* In spite of its factual errors, the animated cartoon captures Johnny's light-hearted spirit quite well. It begins with Johnny as a young man working in an apple orchard. Contented and happy, he is singing and whistling the now world-famous song "The Lord is Good to Me":[6]

> The Lord is good to me,
> And so I thank the Lord,
> For giving me the things I need
> The sun and rain and an apple seed
> Yes, he's been good to me.

As the Disney version continues, we discover that Johnny is not entirely content. We see him casting longing eyes on the wagon trains heading west, and we hear the people singing,

> Get on a wagon rollin' west,
> Seeking a land that's new.
> Get on a wagon rollin' west,
> There's plenty of room for you.

Johnny wishes that he could go along, but he believes that he is too little and too weak to do so. After all, he is "just a sawed-off, scrawny little fella." Wonderfully, his guardian angel shows up and encourages him to go out west if that's his choice. But Johnny says,

> Why don't I go west?
> 'Cuz I ain't got the muscle or the breadth of chest.
> Out there it's the strong men who survive
> And I'm about the puniest fella alive.

Johnny's ever-optimistic guardian angel assures him that he is fully adequate to meet the challenge. Looking beyond Johnny's outward features, he says, "You've got faith and courage and a level head." In addition, he says that Johnny has an important service to perform—planting and growing apple trees:

> So pack your stuff and get a goin'
> Get them apple trees a growin'
> There's a lot of work out there to do
> There's a lot of work to do!

Johnny has everything he needs. He has faith and courage, a level head, and an important service to provide. But Johnny hesitates, still unsure of himself. He says,

> I ain't got the traps.
> I ain't got the gear.
> Or none of the things
> I'll need out there.

The angel refuses to be put off by Johnny's resistance. Instead, he continues to encourage him, showing him the gear he already has: his bag of seeds, his Bible, and his cooking pot:

> Dad gummit, boy, I'm ashamed of you
> You've got the stuff to see you through.
> You've got all the seeds you're needin'
> And for pretty darn good readin'
> There ain't nothin' finer then your book.
> Here's a mighty handy bonnet,
> Even got a handle on it,
> Turn it upside down and you can cook!

Putting his arm around Johnny's shoulder, the angel urges Johnny to get started:

> So come on son and get a-goin'
> Get them apple trees a growin' . . .

Johnny is now thoroughly convinced. Happy and delighted, he strides off, side by side with his guardian angel, as they sing together,

There's a lot of work out there to do
Oh, there's a lot of work to do.

As the story develops we see Johnny befriending the animals, the settlers, and the American Indians, showing partiality to no person or thing. Even a little skunk, on an assignment to spray Johnny, changes his mind when he comes into Johnny's presence. Instead of spraying him, he rolls onto his back, holds up his paws like a kitten, and smiles contentedly as Johnny scratches his tummy. All along we hear the melody of the theme song: "The Lord is good to me, and so I thank the Lord . . ."

In the end, after a lifetime of love and service, Johnny is again visited by his guardian angel, who tells him that he is now needed in heaven to plant more apple trees. As always, Johnny is delighted by the prospect of being useful. He travels off for his final adventure—planting apple trees in heaven.

The Disney version of the Johnny Appleseed story may have mixed up some of the facts: for example, Johnny was not "puny,"[7] and he was not from Pittsburgh. However, they were right about the most important parts of Johnny's story—his joy, his gentleness, his ability to get along with everyone, his belief in angels, and his devotion to useful service. All in all, the writers, directors, and producers have done the world an enormous amount of good in capturing these qualities for the viewing and listening pleasure of future generations.

Wonderfully, whenever and wherever people sing the familiar table blessing "The Lord is Good to Me," they can remember Johnny Appleseed, the gentle pioneer who did not come to conquer the frontier, kill its animals, or subdue its people. Instead, he came to cooperate with the land, enjoy its beauty, and coexist with everyone. He was, indeed, a different kind of hero.

John Chapman's Faith

Most books and movies about Johnny Appleseed have been written for children and appropriately focus on his kindness toward nature, animals, and people. While they often mention that he carried a Bible, they say little about the animating force of his life—his profound religious belief. More specifically, they sometimes mention his love for the teachings of Emanuel Swedenborg, but say little about it.

However, in order to fully understand Johnny Appleseed it is important to understand his faith. As biographer Howard Means puts it, religion was "the core of his being."[8]

As we shall see in subsequent chapters, John Chapman was a devoted reader of Emanuel Swedenborg (1688–1772) and an avid disseminator of his writings. In *Melody Time,* Johnny's angel says that the Bible is "darn good readin'." Swedenborg would agree. In fact, he wrote twenty-five thick Latin volumes to show what "darn good readin'" he believed the Bible really is.

To a great extent, the frontier Christianity of Johnny's day was based on a very harsh and literal interpretation of the Bible. Fire and brimstone preachers like Jonathan Edwards (1703–58) taught that we are all "sinners in the hands of an angry God." They terrified their listeners with vivid descriptions of a fiercely angry God who was determined to let them all burn in eternal hellfire. Johnny, however, was open to a more loving and sensible interpretation—just the kind of interpretation that Swedenborg provides.

According to Swedenborg, God is pure love. Therefore it is impossible for God to be angry or even exhibit sternness.[9] Moreover, all people, whether they worship God or the Great Spirit, whether they live in a log cabin, a wigwam, or an igloo, are children of the same Creator. Everyone who is born has an equal chance of going to heaven.[10] We go there every time we think a noble thought, and we stay there when it becomes our nature to love others more than ourselves.[11]

In other words, the question of who goes to heaven does not depend upon a particular faith system or one's religious affiliation. Rather, it's about *how* we live our life, and *why* we do what we do.[12] In other words, it's about what's in our hearts and minds—our essential character. Johnny's angel, for example, was looking at Johnny's spiritual core, not his religion, and certainly not his external features: "You've got faith and courage and a level head," he said. According to Swedenborg, this is exactly what angels do—they see the best in us.[13] In the Bible (the book that Johnny's angel says is "pretty darn good readin'") there is a similar statement: "Man looks at the outward appearance, but the Lord looks at the heart" (1 Samuel 16:7).

Swedenborg also emphasizes the importance of service. "The kingdom of heaven," he writes, "is a kingdom of useful service."[14] For Swedenborg, true faith and useful service are one.

In the Disney cartoon, Johnny's angel appears to be echoing this idea when he reminds Johnny that *there's a lot of work to do.*

Early receivers of Swedenborg's teachings treated them with the greatest respect. The French writer Honoré de Balzac (1799–1850) said that "Swedenborg undoubtedly epitomizes all the religions—or rather the one religion of humanity." The Scottish historian Thomas Carlyle (1795–1881) wrote of Swedenborg, "More truths are confessed in his writings than in those of any other man." And the American Quaker poet John Greenleaf Whittier (1807–1892) said that Swedenborg's revelations "look through all external and outward manifestations to inward realities . . . literally unmasking the universe and laying bare the profoundest mysteries of life."

"Seekin' a Land That's New"

Many of the talented researchers who have devoted substantial time and energy to uncovering the true story of Johnny Appleseed have not been students of Swedenborg. Admittedly, it takes many years and thoughtful study to thoroughly understand Swedenborg's theology. While the basics are simple (love God, love your neighbor), the explanations are complex and vast. This is perhaps why Ralph Waldo Emerson (1803–82) was inspired to say, "The most remarkable step in the religious history of recent ages is that made by the genius of Swedenborg. A colossal soul, he lies vast abroad of his times, uncomprehended by them, and requires a long focal distance to be seen. . . . He is not to be measured by whole colleges of ordinary scholars."[15]

In some cases, the inability to fully comprehend Swedenborg's theology has resulted in mistaken ideas about the true nature of Johnny Appleseed. Scholars have conjectured about why he never married, why he lived in the woods, why he was a vegetarian, why he wouldn't harm a mosquito, and why he wore a cooking pot on his head. Their conclusions are based on stories that have been handed down through the generations. For the most part, these stories are childhood impressions and dim recollections, passed down in a historical version of "whisper down the lane." And many are "tall tales" told merely to amuse children, but later retold as fact.[16]

To reason about Johnny in this way is to draw conclusions based on his outward appearance and not on his essence. It would be like judging a book by its cover, an apple by its peel, or a person by a story about them. In this book, we will go beyond the outward appearance and take a new look at Johnny Appleseed. We will examine the peel (what people saw), enjoy the fruit (what he did), and discover *the core of Johnny Appleseed* (who he really was). This wagon is ready to roll . . .

> So get on a wagon rollin' west,
> Seekin' a land that's new.
> Get on a wagon rollin' west,
> There's plenty of room for you!

2

The Peel

(What People Saw)

Thinking from the eye closes understanding,
but thinking from understanding opens the eye.

—Emanuel Swedenborg, *Divine Love and Wisdom* 46

Spring Blossoms or Autumn Leaves

The births of legendary people, whether real or fictional, are often shrouded in folklore. It is said, for example, that when the fictional hero Paul Bunyan was born, he was already so big that it took five storks to deliver him to his parents. The Buddha is said to have been born under a cascade of falling blossoms. Later on, wherever the baby Buddha walked, lotus flowers sprung up in his footsteps.

There is a similar story surrounding the birth of Johnny Appleseed. On the day that Johnny Appleseed was born, it is said, apple blossoms, gently blowing in the April breeze, reached down and tapped on his bedroom window. Delighted by nature's welcome, little Johnny spontaneously reached up and tried to touch the beautiful flowers.[1]

Even the most basic information about Johnny's origins is confused and contradictory. Some said he was born in Springfield, Massachusetts. Others favored Boston. One source called him "a stray Yankee from Connecticut."[2] According to some reports, he hailed from Pennsylvania. However, Maryland and Ohio were also strong contenders for his birthplace. The surprising thing is that most of these claims were reported in reputable newspapers and magazines.

Another uncertainty that troubled early Appleseed scholars was the question of his ancestry. Some claimed simply that his parentage was unknown; others said that his father was a settler and his mother an American Indian (or vice versa). And in one fictional account, he is described as the son of a Massachusetts minister who later sent him to be educated at Harvard College.

In 1939, Florence Wheeler, who served as the librarian in Leominster, Massachusetts, discovered genealogical records that shed new light on the legend and lore surrounding Johnny's birth. She wrote: "Our church and civic records record the marriage of Nathaniel Chapman and Elizabeth Simons, Feb. 8, 1770. Elizabeth was the daughter of James Simons, a prosperous farmer whose house was on the corner of what is now Maple and West Street."[3]

In addition, Miss Wheeler discovered that Johnny's paternal ancestors came from Yorkshire, England, and settled in Boston in 1639. His mother was a direct descendent of William Simonds Sr., who had arrived in Boston harbor in 1635. Interestingly, and perhaps prophetically, William Simonds came to America on a ship called the *Planter*.[4]

Miss Wheeler also found the birth dates for Nathaniel and Elizabeth's children:

ELIZABETH CHAPMAN, *born* NOVEMBER 18, 1770
(named after her mother)

JOHN CHAPMAN, *born* SEPTEMBER 26, 1774
(named after his grandfather)

NATHANIEL CHAPMAN, JR., *born* JUNE 26, 1776
(named after his father)

The evidence is now in. John (not "Jonathan") Chapman, the second child and first son of Nathaniel and Elizabeth Chapman, was born in Leominster, Massachusetts, on September 26, 1774. Late September in Massachusetts is time for autumn leaves and apple picking, not April breezes and spring blossoms, a fact that must replace the sweet but mistaken legend of the apple blossoms tapping Johnny's window when he was born.

Early Years

On September 21, 1774, just five days before John Chapman was born, an urgent call went out announcing that all able-bodied men between the ages of sixteen and sixty should be prepared for the possibility of military duty. Because these men were told to be ready at a moment's notice, they came to be known as the "minutemen." As stated in the original resolution, "Resolved that it be hereby recommended to the Militia in all Parts of this Colony, to hold themselves in Readiness to march at a Minute's Warning, to the Relief of Any Place that may be attacked."

Revolutionary War military records reveal that Nathaniel Chapman, John's father, was twenty-eight years old and five feet nine inches tall when he enlisted as a minuteman. In April 1775, when Johnny was seven months old, Nathaniel Chapman left for Lexington, and in June of that same year fought in the historic battle of Bunker Hill. Over the next five years, he continued to serve as a soldier in General George Washington's army, and was elevated to the rank of captain. He only visited home on rare occasions.

On one of those visits, sometime during the month of October 1775, Elizabeth became pregnant with their third child. It was a difficult pregnancy. Elizabeth was ill most of the time, and without her husband, who had returned to military service. As the time of birth approached, Elizabeth wrote a poignant letter to Nathaniel. The letter is dated June 3, 1776. Retaining the original spelling and punctuation, and with a few additions [in brackets] to aid comprehension, the letter reads as follows:

Loving Husband,

These lines come with my affectionate regards to you hoping they will find you in health, tho I still continue in a very weak and low condition. I am no better than I was when you left me but rather worse, and I should be very glad if you could come and see me for I want to see you.

Our children are both well thro the Divine Goodness.

I have received but two letters from you since you went away—neither knew where you was till last Friday I [received] one, and [the following] Sabbathday evening another, and I rejoice to hear that you are well and I pray you may thus continue and in God's due time be returned in safety. I send this letter by Mr. Mullins and I hope it will reach you and I should be glad if you would send me a letter back by him.

I have wrote that I should be glad you come to see me if you could, but if you cannot, I desire you should make yourself as easy as possible for I am under the care of a kind Providence who is able to do more for me than I can ask or think and I desire humbly to submit to His Holy Will with patience and resignation, patiently to bear what he shall see fitt to lay upon me. My cough is something abated, but I think I grow weaker. I desire your prayers for me that I may be prepared for the will of God that I may so improve my remainder of life that I may answer the great end for which I was made, that I might glorify God here and finally come to the enjoyment of Him in a world of glory, thro the merits of Jesus Christ.

Remember, I beseech you, that you are a mortall and that you must submit to death sooner or later and consider that we are always in danger of our spiritual enemy. Be, therefore, on your guard continually, and live in daily preparation for death—and so I must bid you farewell and if it should be so ordered that I should not see you again, I hope we shall both be as happy as to spend an eternity of happiness together in the coming world which is my desire and prayer.

So I conclude by subscribing myself, your
Ever loving and affectionate wife

Elizabeth Chapman[5]

There is no record of this letter ever being answered; nor did Nathaniel Chapman, who was twenty-nine and away on military duty, return home to witness the birth of his son. Three weeks later, Elizabeth gave birth to her third child, Nathaniel Jr. But the long sickness had taken its toll on the young mother. On July 18, 1776, at the age of twenty-eight, Elizabeth Chapman died, presumably of tuberculosis. Two weeks later, her baby died as well.

Johnny was almost two years old at the time of the family tragedy, and his sister would be six in November. For the next four years, Elizabeth and Johnny were taken in by relatives in the Leominster area while they waited for their father to return from military service. In the summer of 1780, when Johnny was nearly six and Elizabeth nearly ten, their father completed his military duty and came home. In that same summer Captain Nathaniel Chapman moved his family to Longmeadow, Massachusetts, and on July 24 he married Lucy Cooley.[6]

Longmeadow was Lucy's hometown, situated adjacent to Springfield and on the eastern bank of the Connecticut River. It was there, in the Longmeadow school system, that John Chapman first learned the ornate copperplate script that he used on the many deeds and transactions of his later business career. Longmeadow's picturesque fields and streams also gave him an opportunity to appreciate the world of nature. Situated in a beautiful valley on the Connecticut River, Longmeadow was an ideal place for young Johnny Appleseed to cultivate his love for the great outdoors.

On July 13, 1787, when Johnny was just twelve years old, the Northwest Ordinance was enacted. This was a plan for United States expansion into the unclaimed territories beyond the

Allegheny Mountains. While Johnny may not have been aware of the politics behind the plan, he most certainly would have been aware of the many pioneers and wagon trains that were passing through Longmeadow on the well-worn "Connecticut Path"—a trail that stretched from Boston to Albany.

Excitement was in the air! The prospect of great adventures beyond the mountains beckoned to many. Something was stirring. We can imagine young Johnny dreaming of the time when he too would be heading westward into the newly opened territories.

The Chapman Brothers Leave Home

In 1781, Lucy Cooley Chapman gave birth to her first child, Nathaniel, named after his father. Over the next twenty years (1783–1803), she would give birth to nine more children. Counting Johnny and his older sister, there were twelve children in the household.

In 1797, when Johnny was twenty-three years old and his younger brother, Nathaniel, was sixteen, they headed west. While the documentation is not conclusive, there is a strong likelihood that the Chapman brothers traveled beyond the western border of Massachusetts, followed the Connecticut Path westward, spent time in Wilkes-Barre, Pennyslvania, along the Susquehanna River, and then crossed the rugged Allegheny Mountains, finally settling near the Allegheny River, perhaps in the town of Warren in western Pennsylvania.[7]

It was during this time period that Johnny wrote a brief promissory note to either his father or his half-brother; the note simply names "Nathaniel Chapman." The IOU has become the first actual documentation of the transition from John Chapman, the traveling youngster from Massachusetts, to the man who would later be known as Johnny Appleseed, the legendary nurseryman of the new West. The now-famous note is important because it gives a definite time and place for locating Johnny. The note reads as follows:

> Franklin, February 4, 1804, for value received I promise to pay Nathaniel Chapman [on] order the sum of one hundred dollars in land or apple trees with interest till paid as witness my hand.
>
> John Chapman[8]

This is the first recorded documentation of Johnny's business transactions that we have. But it does not mean that Johnny waited until 1804 to start his nursery business. After all, he was now thirty years old, and had been away from home for seven years. In all likelihood, Johnny may have spent many years going back and forth on the Allegheny River between Warren, Franklin, and Pittsburgh, even going as far south as the cider mills of Brownsville, doing business and buying provisions.

One of the most famous and memorable sightings of this time period is recorded by William Glines, a man who knew the Chapman brothers personally. The scene that he describes takes place along the Allegheny River sometime between 1797 and

1800. Johnny is in his mid-twenties and his brother Nathaniel is in his late teens. Glines writes:

> During the winter, Johnny wanted to go down the river a short distance, and as the ice was running, he concluded to take a small canoe they had procured and started on his journey, but finding it rather troublesome to keep the canoe right side up, he concluded to drag the canoe to the center of a large strong cake of ice.
>
> Having succeeded, he laid down in the canoe, made himself as comfortable as he could, went to sleep and when he awoke found himself about 100 miles below where he intended to stop.
>
> He, however, returned to his brother who had suffered much during Johnny's long delay.[9]

Whether historically accurate or not, this picture reveals many things about Johnny's nature. It speaks of his resourcefulness, his courage, his phenomenal ability to endure harsh conditions, and his lack of anxiety, a gift that allowed him to sleep through difficulties.

Later, as the legend of Johnny Appleseed grew, there would be more stories about Johnny's amazing abilities. In one of the more enduring stories it is said that he was so tough that he could melt ice with his bare feet. Apparently, Johnny's younger brother, Nathaniel, was not endowed with the same survival skills. In one case, Johnny had to go off in search of provisions, leaving his brother alone in their winter cabin for four weeks. According to Glines:

The country being new and unsettled they often suffered for want of the necessaries of life. Johnny finally concluded that he must go to Pittsburgh for provisions, and leave his brother to do the best he could; he said one would live there better than two, unless they had more provision. At length he left his young brother to look out for himself. . . . During Johnny's absence, Nathaniel became very much reduced and must have starved to death, but for a tribe of Indians who were wandering through the country who found and relieved him of his suffering; they taught him the uses of the bow and arrow to success in killing small game.[10]

Sometime after 1804, when Nathaniel was around twenty-three, he and Johnny decided to go their separate ways. It could be that Nathaniel needed to go ahead to Ohio to make arrangements for his father, mother, and nine siblings, who had decided to leave Longmeadow and resettle in the west.[11] Or it could be that Nathaniel realized that he was no longer able to keep up with the rugged ways of his older brother, Johnny Appleseed.

Personal Appearance and Character Traits

Perhaps the most striking and often noted thing about Johnny's personal appearance is the intensity and brilliance of his eyes. People would remark that "his keen, black eyes sparkled with a peculiar brightness."[12] There was something inescapably moving about his powerful gaze: "he had extraordinarily brilliant eyes, dark and piercing."[13] He would launch into a sermon based on something he read in Swedenborg with "black eyes blazing."[14]

Especially when he spoke about the wonders of nature, and how they revealed the glory of God, his eyes would become fiery: "Eyes blazing, Johnny Appleseed would show you how to see the divine in nature."[15]

His voice, too, commanded attention. An elderly woman recalls the effect that Johnny's words had on her, even as a child.

> I saw him once at the table, when I was very small, telling about some apples that were new to us. His description was poetical, the language remarkably well-chosen; it could have been no finer had the whole of Webster's Unabridged, with all its royal vocabulary, been fresh upon his ready tongue. I stood back at mother's chair, amazed, delighted, bewildered, and vaguely realizing the wonderful powers of true oratory.[16]

Johnny's "true oratory" was without pretentiousness or pride: "His diction was pure and chaste, and his language simple but grammatical."[17] He would at times "burst into a startling inspiration of eloquence, complete and consummate, exalted, beautiful."[18] As a result, "He penetrated his auditors, apparently without intending to do so, and moved them without knowing it."[19]

These same sources describe Johnny as being "an exceedingly vigorous soul," "packed full of Yankee energy," and "full of restless activity." The vital force burned so brightly in him that it is said that "he crossed Lake Erie on the ice barefooted," while others who attempted to do the same thing froze to death. He could do the work of two men, walk thousands of miles on foot, and plant apple trees "over a hundred thousand square miles of territory."[20]

And yet he is also described as "fond of ease," someone who could enjoy simply "laying in the shade of a spreading tree" or "dozing off in the midst of the most dangerous circumstances."[21] A delightful example of Johnny's easygoing attitude, even in risky situations, is given by Anne Eliot Crompton. In her book *Johnny's Trail,* which she describes as "almost true," Johnny is telling a young person about his narrow escape from the Wyandot Indians:

> One time I was running from those fellows, those Wyandots . . . Couldn't shake them. Had to walk into a pondful of cattails and lie down amongst [them].
>
> The Wyandots came up, splashed around searching. One of them darn near stepped on me. But I was well down in the water by then, breathing through a straw. When they went off, I didn't dare come up. Had a nice long nap down there in the reeds.[22]

According to the legend, then, Johnny Appleseed could sleep through danger, exhibiting what Hemingway once called "grace under pressure." Of course, this could also be another "Johnny story."

One of the most endearing pictures of Johnny Appleseed is the description of his first entrance into Ohio. Reminiscent of the way he is said to have floated down the Allegheny a few years before, sleeping on a cake of ice, he is now seen on a summer day, drifting lazily down the Ohio River. He is resting in the dugout of a hollowed-out log, "snoozing without a care in the world, evidently trusting in the river to take him wherever it was he wanted to go."[23]

Johnny's carefree, fun-loving nature is also apparent in the stories that circulated about his playful ways. For example, on one occasion someone noticed that he had bought a complete set of dishes. When someone asked him why he needed so many dishes, he said, "Well that way I won't have to do dishes till the end of the week." In reality, he was buying them as a gift for a poor housewife![24]

While the classic caricature of Johnny Appleseed pictures him as a man in ragged clothes with a cooking pot sitting sideways on his head, it's not certain whether he ever actually did this. If he did, it's most likely that he put the pot on his head in a cock-eyed manner to amuse children—not to free up space while traveling.[25]

The ragged clothing, however, was indeed an aspect of his outward appearance. "Johnny may not have been well dressed, even by frontier standards . . . His trousers were short and frazzled at the bottom with briars and burrs, and were supported in some half-hearted fashion by some original substitute for suspenders."[26] He spent no time shopping for new clothes: "His clothing was mostly old, given to him in exchange for apple trees."[27]

In his later years he sported "a coffee-sack, in which he cut holes for his head and arms to pass through." He said that it was "a very serviceable cloak, and as good clothing as any man need wear."[28] Moreover, it was not unusual for people to cut a hole in a blanket, pull it over one's head, and use it as a coat.

Nor was it unusual for people to go shoeless in those days.

While stories abound about Johnny's rejection of shoes even in the midst of winter "as a matter of conscience,"[29] these are surely exaggerations. It is true that "generally, even in the coldest weather, he went barefooted." But it should also be noted that "sometimes, for his long journeys, he would make himself a rude pair of sandals."[30]

In the August 1859 issue of *Harper's Magazine,* there is an editorial about a Dartmouth College professor who notices a farmer "trudging along the dusty street barefooted and coatless." Disdaining the farmer's unsightly appearance, the well-dressed professor growls, "I should like to know if all the people of East Hanover go barefoot." The barefoot farmer replies, "Part of 'em do, and the rest of 'em mind their own business!"[31]

"You, Johnny, Are Always Welcome"

Among the most popular "Johnny" stories—far more endearing than the portrayals of him as a ragged, barefooted, and pot-headed vagabond—are the stories that reveal "the native goodness of his heart."[32] While many of the stories are exaggerated and some are improbable, there is a core of truth within them that tells us a great deal about Johnny Appleseed.

For example, Johnny enjoyed carrying presents with him when he came to visit: "In his pack, Johnny would sometimes carry a present of tea for some housewife who needed a bit of cheer." Similarly, "he would carry a piece of bright calico or a gay ribbon for a child who had saved seeds for him during the winter."[33] His arrival was always an occasion for joy: "He could tell the most engaging stories; he could whistle and sing the gayest tunes; he could care for a childish hurt in the tenderest way."[34]

His kindness was not limited to the children of settlers. He was also welcome among the American Indians and beloved by their children. This is depicted in a delightful issue of *Classic Illustrated Junior* comics (1955) in which Johnny stops to visit with the American Indians for the night. As he enters the village, he is immediately surrounded by the children, who all want his attention. A smiling squaw, with a papoose on her back, says, "You, Johnny, are always welcome."[35]

On the very next page, Johnny is pictured giving a cup of water to a wounded brave who is resting under a tree. The brave has bandages on his arm and across his chest. Apparently, Johnny has provided the bandages and is serving as a healer. A few feet away, in the same picture, a settler is sitting against a rock, holding his bandaged head—another of Johnny's grateful patients. In the background, enveloped in a hazy, discolored cloud, settlers and American Indians are furiously clashing. The heading for the picture is as follows:

> Whenever there was a battle between the settlers and the Indians, Johnny was always there. But not to fight. His heart told him that fighting was wrong. Instead, he braved the whizzing arrows and bullets to give aid to the wounded, Indian and settler alike. All men were God's children to Johnny Appleseed. He did not take sides.[36]

Kindness to Animals

Stories abound about Johnny Appleseed's kindness to animals. Again, we need to search for the elements of truth amid popular legends. One of the more famous is a story about how he found an old wolf caught in a trap. He not only freed the wolf, but also bandaged its leg, treating it so kindly that the wolf eventually followed Johnny around like a puppy.

In another story, Johnny was about to make a fire for himself at the end of a giant hollowed-out log. Suddenly he noticed that a mother bear and her cubs were already sleeping in the log. Johnny put out his fire, preferring to sleep in the cold rather than disturb them. In a different version, it's a mother chipmunk and her babies, not a mother bear and her cubs. They have settled into a hollow log for a night's sleep, the same log that Johnny had selected for his own slumbers. In this version, instead of shooing away the chipmunk and her babies, Johnny gives up his berth in the hollow log and chooses to sleep in the *snow*—not just in the cold!

And then there are the stories about Johnny's compassion for every living thing, even ants and mosquitoes. In one story Johnny attempts

to cook a hot meal for himself. After getting a good fire going, he notices that mosquitoes are flying into the fire and dying. Because of his great love for every creature, even the lowliest insect, he puts out the fire and eats a cold supper.[37]

Admittedly, these stories strain credulity. It may be possible to tame a wolf, but ordinarily this takes place over many generations. It is conceivable that Johnny was so much in tune with nature that a mother bear would not feel defensive in his presence, but this takes what literary critics call "a willing suspension of disbelief." It makes sense that Johnny would put out a fire if it were attracting mosquitoes, especially if he did not want to be stung, but to suggest that he was a nonviolent Hindu saint, or a pantheist who would not kill living things because he believed them to be part of God, does not square with what we know about his religious beliefs.

We can, however, say this: his years of experience in the wilderness, his God-given compassion, and his innate ability to understand the language of nature gave Johnny Appleseed the ability to live cooperatively with animals and in harmony with his environment. He was not only aware of nature's beauty, but also sensitive to its rhythms and needs.

Johnny's natural compassion gave him a certain kinship with the animals. If he heard that an animal was being mistreated or abused, he would purchase it and then pay another settler to take care of it until it regained its health. At that point, the settler could keep the animal or sell it to someone else who would take good care of it.

Johnny was especially concerned about abandoned horses: "It frequently happened that the long journey into the wilderness would cause the new settlers to be encumbered with lame and broken-down horses that were turned loose to die."[38] Whenever Johnny saw this, or heard about it, he refused to let the horses be slaughtered, abandoned, or mistreated in any way. Instead, he would make arrangements for their care and shelter with local settlers, paying them for their efforts. When the horses recovered, Johnny gave them to needy families, under the condition that the horses would be treated well. As one person recalls, "he was never known to hurt any animal or give pain to any living thing."[39]

In brief, Johnny was one of those rare individuals who did not believe that the world belonged to him; rather, he believed that he belonged to the world.[40] And he proved it by his life, immortalized, and often exaggerated, in the legends that followed him—many of which he may have started himself!

3

The Fruit

(What Johnny Did)

You shall know them by their fruits. —Matthew 7:16

A Moveable Enterprise

Johnny's initial work in western Pennsylvania was just the beginning of a long and memorable career. His labors over the next forty-five years (1800–45) would extend beyond Pennsylvania into Ohio and eventually into Indiana, all of which became known as "Johnny Appleseed Country." In some accounts, because of the seeds that Johnny gave to settlers traveling west, "Appleseed Country" extended even to Illinois, Kentucky, and beyond.

But in order to appreciate this aspect of the Johnny Appleseed story, we need to start at the beginning, in western Pennsylvania, where Johnny was planting the first of his many nurseries. One of the earliest recollections on record is given by a man named R. I. Curtis, who wrote in 1859: "I knew him in Venango County, Pennsylvania, nearly sixty years ago [around 1800] when I was a child of eight or nine years."[1]

Curtis reports that Johnny "subsisted one whole winter on butternuts." He then reveals important details about how Johnny conducted his apple tree enterprise. According to Curtis, Johnny was already anticipating those places where he believed "at a future day apple trees would be wanted." Johnny traveled from Venango County south toward Pittsburgh, a hundred-mile journey along the Allegheny River, in order to harvest seeds from the cider mills near Pittsburgh. As Curtis puts it, "Then, in the fall, he would repair to [i.e., travel to] Allegheny County, Pennsylvania, and wash out of the pomace at cider mills a bushel or two of seeds, and return with them on his shoulder, plant them at the proper time, enclose the spot with a brush fence, and pay some attention to the cultivation."[2]

Here we have, in a nutshell, the rudimentary form of the plan that would become the hallmark of Johnny Appleseed's entrepreneurial career. He would first select a spot where he anticipated a need for apple trees; then, after harvesting seeds from the leftover pulp at cider mills, he would return to plant and cultivate his nursery, eventually selling seedlings and saplings to settlers who would be moving into the area.

Johnny's idea was not new; many others were in the business of gathering seeds at the cider presses in larger cities and starting nurseries in the area. What was new, however, was that Johnny conceived the idea of a moveable enterprise. In other words, as the frontier continued to move west, so would Johnny, always anticipating where the early pioneers might choose to settle. There he would plant his apple nursery, hire someone to tend it, and move on, further into the frontier, to plant more nurseries. Occasionally he would return to check his fences, cultivate his plantings, and meet with his workers, but he was always looking ahead, planning ahead, moving ahead to the next location. By the time the settlers arrived, Johnny's seedlings and saplings would be well developed and ready for sale.

The Need for Apples on the Frontier

In 1929, the Daughters of the American Revolution presented to the state of Ohio an *Official Roster of the Soldiers of the American Revolution*

Apple tree order with Johnny's signature

Buried in the State of Ohio. The roster is dedicated "To the Pioneers of Ohio who Served their Country in the Revolutionary War," and contains the following preamble:

> Lest the reader should wonder at the large number of Revolutionary soldiers buried in Ohio, it should be recalled that the present boundaries of Ohio were nearest the original colonies, and when land grants were given to the soldiers, thither came the hardy New Englanders to the Western Reserve and the region of Lake Erie; sturdy Pennsylvanians crossed over into central Ohio and the Virginian and Carolinian took up his abode in the southern part of Ohio. Here in the Northwest Territory they lived and died; they were fathers of a race who inherited the invincible courage and sterling qualities

of the Revolutionary soldier and who took up the burden of founding the Nation by pressing westward.[3]

Among other things, this document tells us that land grants were given to the veterans of the Revolutionary War. This would include Johnny's father, Captain Nathaniel Chapman, who served as a quartermaster in General George Washington's army.[4] Captain Chapman, together with his wife and children, migrated to Ohio in 1805 and resettled on Duck Creek, about fifteen miles north of Marietta. The publication produced by the Daughters of the American Revolution, listing the names of those soldiers who were buried in Ohio, included Johnny's father:

CHAPMAN, NATHANIEL (Columbiana Co.)
    Capt. of Company of Wheelwrights. Br. 1740, Springfield, Mass. Mar Lucy Cooley. D 1807, Salem, O. Ref : Natl No 59467 p 159, Vol. 00, D. A. R. Lin.[5]

According to this record, Captain Nathaniel Chapman was born in 1740 (actually it was 1746), married Lucy Cooley in Springfield, Massachusetts, and died in 1807. The old soldier lived only two years in Ohio, dying at the age of sixty. Three years later, his wife, Lucy Cooley Chapman, also passed away.

Meanwhile, Johnny continued to serve his country, not as a soldier, but as a nurseryman. He was thirty-three at the time of his father's passing, and in the midst of a booming business opportunity. The Northwest Ordinance had opened for settlement the entire territory north of the Ohio River up to the Great Lakes, and eastward to the Mississippi River—an area that today includes Ohio, Indiana, Illinois, Michigan, and Wisconsin. The ordinance also contained the requirement that everyone who purchased land in this newly opened territory, or received a land grant, *had to plant fifty apple or pear trees within the first three years.* This was to discourage real estate speculation and assure that the land would be used for its intended purpose—for settlement.

Selling apple seedlings to the settlers proved to be a perfect business for Johnny, not just because fifty fruit trees were required for proof of land ownership, but also because apple trees were essential for survival on the frontier. They grew well and had a wide variety of uses. They could be eaten directly from the tree; they could be used to make pies, dumplings, fritters and pancakes; they could be baked, boiled, fried, turned into chips and chutney, churned into butter, or made into sauce. Apple cider vinegar was especially important as a preservative for other foods and as an antiseptic. The apples themselves were extremely hardy; they could be easily stored in a root cellar and used throughout the long winter. And, of course, there was always apple juice, apple cider, applejack, and apple brandy—all of which were considered staples on the American frontier.

The demand for apples, therefore, was high, and the need was great—not only to secure title to one's property but also to subsist as a settler. But not everyone had the seeds, the knowhow, or the time to plant fifty trees. Enter Johnny Appleseed. He had

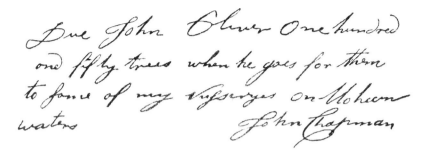

IOU with Johnny's signature

all of those things. Because of this, he was able to provide the newly arrived pioneers with young seedlings that would soon start bearing fruit. Having seedlings (and saplings) that would soon become fruit-bearing trees was a real advantage for settlers who needed to make use of their fruit trees as soon as possible.

For Johnny Appleseed, apple trees were a cash crop; for the settlers, they were essential for survival. There is no doubt that his presence was a godsend to many.

Living the Good Life

One of the most precious stories of this time period is recorded in a letter written by a gentleman named E. Vandorn in 1873.

The letter, which contains a fond reminiscence of meeting Johnny, explains that when Johnny planted larger nurseries, he would need something more than a temporary shelter in which to live. In those cases, he would build a small log cabin and invite neighbors to assist him. Vandorn recalls his experience when he and his brother Cornelius traveled through the woods to help Johnny. When they arrived, it was toward the end of the day, and Johnny was already preparing his supper:

In the dusk of the evening we saw smoke curling up amongst the tree tops, and directly we saw Johnny standing close to a fire kindled by the side of a large log, an old tree which had been torn up by the roots.

I never shall forget how pleased he appeared to be when we came up to him in the wilderness . . . among bears, wolves, catamounts, serpents, owls and porcupines, yet apparently contented and supremely happy. . . .

After sitting down and chatting for a while, Johnny poked in the ashes with a stick and dragged out some potatoes, saying, "This is the way I live in the wilderness. . . . I could not enjoy myself better anywhere—I can lay on my back, look up at the stars and it seems almost as though I can see the angels praising God, for he has made all things good."[6]

The reminiscence concludes with the boys opening their sack and sharing their provisions with Johnny—dried venison, bread, and butter. Johnny eats some of the bread and butter while they enjoy hot potatoes seasoned with salt.

Apparently, Johnny knew how to lead "the good life."

A Fruitful Life

Johnny's moveable business continued to grow and flourish throughout the remaining years of his life. The story of his final years of faithful service is preserved in the historical records of Crawford County, Ohio: "He was frequently seen here by the early settlers, and nine out of ten of the early orchards here are said to have originated from his nurseries."[7]

After summarizing his early years in Massachusetts and Pennsylvania, the historical account continues:

> Years afterward, when the hardy pioneers from Western
> Virginia and Pennsylvania scaled the Allegheny Moun-
> tains and sought homes in the valleys of Ohio, they found
> the little nurseries of seedling apple trees on Braddock's
> Field, at Wheeling Creek, the Flats of Grave Creek, Holi-
> day's Cove, and at other places along the Ohio Valley. . . .
> In 1838—thirty-seven years after his appearance on Licking
> Creek—Johnny noticed that civilization, wealth and popula-
> tion were pressing into the wilderness of Ohio. Hitherto he
> had easily kept just in advance of the wave of settlement . . .
> [now] he felt that his work was done in the region in which
> he had labored so long.

In just thirty-seven years, the population of Ohio had swelled from forty thousand people to nearly a million. It was time for Johnny to move on. And so in 1840 he moved to Fort Wayne, Indiana, where he continued to plant and sell seedlings.

The Crawford County report then dips back into an 1871 *Harper's* article (published ten years earlier), resurrecting the Bunyanesque story of Johnny's labors: "In the summer of 1847 [actually it was March 18, 1845] when his labors had literally borne fruit over a hundred thousand miles of terri-tory," Johnny Appleseed closed his eyes for the last time. As the report nears its conclusion, it again quotes from the 1871 *Harper's* article:

Declining other accommodations, he slept as usual on the floor, and in the early morning he was found with his features all aglow with a supernal light, and his body so near death that his tongue refused its office. The physician, who was hastily summoned pronounced him dying, but added that he had never seen a man in so placid a state at the approach of death. . . . He ripened into death as naturally and beautifully as the seeds of his own planting had grown into fiber and bud and blossom and the matured fruit.

The Crawford County report is as much a eulogy as an historical record, especially in its closing words: "Thus passed from earth one of the memorable characters of pioneer days, but his memory will linger in the hearts of succeeding generations for years to come, and their children will learn to revere the decaying monuments of his industry and benevolence."[8]

A similar eulogy was given by Senator Sam Houston in an address to the United States Congress.[9] Speaking affectionately of Johnny, the former general said, "This old man was one of the most useful citizens of the world in his humble way. He has made a greater contribution to our civilization than we realize. He has left a place that never can be filled. Farewell, dear old eccentric heart, your labor has been a labor of love, and generations, yet unborn, will rise up and call you blessed."[10]

Johnny Appleseed's labors were, indeed, labors of love, and his contribution to civilization has been a great one. If he could be characterized as a "dear old eccentric heart," perhaps he was so in the same way that Socrates, Galileo, Columbus, and Swedenborg might be considered eccentric—all of whom were well ahead of their time, even as Johnny was well ahead of the settlers, geographically and theologically.[11]

Johnny Appleseed was a brilliant, perceptive, compassionate entrepreneur—a cultural genius, as much at home with pioneer settlers as with American Indians, at ease with children and adults alike, unpretentious and endearing. Moreover, existing legal documents prove that he was a savvy businessman who planted successful nurseries in three states (Pennsylvania, Ohio, and Indiana) and owned at least twenty properties in nineteen counties. This does not include the many nurseries he planted and cultivated on leased and borrowed lands. When he passed on, after a long life of fruitful service, he had owned, at one time or another, over 1,200 acres, many of which contained as many as fifteen thousand seedlings.[12]

On a monument in Dexter City, Ohio, the following words are engraved on a memorial plaque—a fitting tribute to a fruitful life:

Without a Hope of Recompense,
Without a Thought of Pride;
John Chapman Planted Apple Trees,
Preached and Lived and Died.

1774–1845[13]

4

The Core

(Who Johnny Was)

*A good man out of the good treasure
of his heart brings forth good.* —Luke 6:45

"Touched by the Great Spirit"

When Frank O. Chapman addressed the West Virginia Historical Association on April 20, 1967, his topic was Johnny Appleseed. As the great-great-grandson of Johnny's half-brother, Nathaniel Chapman, he had much to say about the "missing pieces" in Johnny's story.

For example, Frank Chapman provided an insight into Johnny's early years in Longmeadow. He said that Johnny, even in his childhood, "loved nature and spent much time along the streams and in the woods. . . . Pet squirrels, rabbits, and birds fearlessly came to him at his whistle or call."[1] Information like this, passed down through the immediate family, seems closer to the truth than stories about rescuing mosquitoes, taming wolves, and sleeping with bears. It also helps us get a fuller picture of who Johnny Appleseed really was.

Frank Chapman also spoke about how the American Indians regarded his famous relative. During the time of the most heated conflicts between pioneer settlers and American Indians, he explained, Johnny managed to earn the respect of everyone. "Johnny knew many Indian chiefs and spoke at least three of the tribal languages," said Chapman. He added that Johnny was so respected by the American Indians that they referred to him as a white man "who had been touched by the Great Spirit."[2]

These simple words reveal something essential about the core of Johnny Appleseed. He was a man of God, touched by the Great Spirit, and so respected among the American Indians that he was invited to join them at their tribal councils.[3]

Discovering Swedenborg

We know that both Johnny and his older sister were baptized in the Congregational Church of Leominster, Massachusetts, on June 25, 1775.[4] On that same day, their parents became members of the church. As mentioned earlier, most churches at that time emphasized the total depravity of man, the fierce anger of God, and the eternal torments of hell. Whether or not this was taught in the Congregational Church that Johnny attended is not known. What is known, though, is that Johnny did not embrace this form of Christianity. Instead, he found himself most at home in an interpretation of Christianity that was much gentler, less fearful, and more forgiving. And he found this in the theological teachings of Emanuel Swedenborg.

The story of how John Chapman discovered the teachings of Emanuel Swedenborg is very much entwined with the story of how the New Church, that is, the church based on Swedenborg's teachings, came to America's shores.

It begins with James Glen, a successful Scottish plantation owner who was sailing from his sugar plantation in South America to England. En route, the captain of the ship, noticing that Glen seemed to be free of religious prejudices, gave him a copy of Swedenborg's *Heaven and Hell.* Robert Hindmarsh, a close friend of James Glen, records what Glen told him about his experience:

> As soon as Mr. Glen had read the work and well considered its contents, he was all astonishment, first, at the nature of the information which that book conveys; and in the next

For the Sentimentalists.

A DISCOURSE

On the Extraordinary SCIENCE of
Celestial and Terrestial Connections and
Correspondencies,

Recently revived, by the late honourable and learned
EMANUEL SWEDENBORG;

Will be delivered by Mr. JAMES GLEN,
an humble pupil and follower of the said Swedenborg's,
At 8 o'clock on the evening of Saturday
the 5th of June 1784, at BELL'S Book-
Store, near St. Paul's Church, in Third-
Street, Philadelphia.

Where Tickets for admittance may now be had, Price
one Quarter Dollar.

THIS sublime science teaches us from every object
in the world of nature to learn things spiritual and
heavenly: It is the most ancient and excellent of all
sciences, being that whereby the holy Scriptures were
written; according to which the highest angels form
their ideas, and through the medium of which the
earliest of the human race, held converse and communication with these blessed beings. The knowledge of
this useful science has for many ages been lost to this
world. The Egyptian hieroglyphics; the Greek and
Roman mythology, and the modern free masonry being the last remnants of it. The honourable Emanuel
Swedenborg the wonderful restorer of this long lost secret, through the Divine Mercy, for the last twenty-
nine years of his life, had the most free and open intercourse with spirits and angels, and was thus taught this
science of heaven. From his invaluable writings and
conversations with gentlemen who have studied them,
the Discourser hopes to convey some idea and taste of
this science of sciences, to the wise and to the good of
every denomination.

According to the following Divisions.

Definition of the Science of
Correspondencies.
Scriptures.
Human Body.
Diseases.
Remedies.
Marriage
Natural Philosophy.
Sun and Moon.
Air.
Earth.
Metals.

Vegetables,
Animals,
Jewish Manners & Customs
Hieroglyphics.
Mythology.
Free Masonry.
Languages.
Character of Nations
Character of Individuals.
Future State.
The Application of the Sci-
ence of Correspondencies.

N. B. A few Copies of Swedenborg's Theosophic Treatise
on the Nature of Influx, as it respects the Communication and Operation of Soul and Body,—May now
be had, at said BELL's Book-store, in Third Street.
Price, two thirds of a Dollar.

JAMES GLEN'S ADVERTISEMENT
FOR HIS PHILADELPHIA LECTURE.

*From Early American Newspapers,
an Archive of Americana Collection,
published by Readex (Readex.com),
a division of NewsBank, Inc.*

place, at the goodness of the Divine Providence which had so unexpectedly brought him into such a peculiar situation, that while sailing on the surface of the great deep, with an abyss of water beneath him, his eyes were opened to behold an abyss of divine truths above and around him. That day Mr. Glen declared to be the happiest day of his life, which thus brought to his view the glories of the heavenly state and the stupendous realities of the eternal world.[5]

A year later, after spending considerable time in London with other "receivers" of Swedenborg's teachings, Glen decided to return to his sugar plantation in South America. Eager to share his discovery with others, he made plans to deliver a lecture about Swedenborg while his ship was making a stopover in Philadelphia. It would be the first public lecture about Emanuel Swedenborg ever given in America.[6]

It was Glen's intention to give a lecture on sacred symbolism, showing how the Bible is written in such a way that everything in nature contains a deeper spiritual meaning. Swedenborg calls this "the knowledge of correspondence." By this he means that everything in the spiritual world has a direct "correspondence" with something in the world of nature. For example, a seed falling on the ground corresponds to truth presented to the human mind. If the seed (truth) falls on good ground (a good heart), it will blossom and bear fruit. The whole process, then, of how a simple seed can become a fruit-bearing tree *in nature* is a living sermon from God about how truth can be received and bear fruit *in human beings*.

Similarly, water, which cleanses the body and refreshes its cells, corresponds to the way spiritual truth—when applied—cleanses the spirit and nourishes the soul. According to Swedenborg, the whole Bible is written in these "correspondences." As Glen put it in his advertisement, "This sublime science teaches us from every object in the world of nature, to learn things spiritual and heavenly." It was Swedenborg's belief that the whole Bible was written in this "most ancient and excellent of all sciences," and that it must be properly understood in order to appreciate the depth and wonder of God's Word.[7]

Glen also wanted to show how Swedenborg's interpretation of Christianity reveals the infinite nature of God's love—a love that knows no wrath, is never angry, and cannot even have a stern countenance. This was quite a contrast to the angry God who was ready to pour out his wrath on depraved sinners.

It should be noted that Glen was appealing to "the sentimentalists"—those whom he called "the wise and good in every

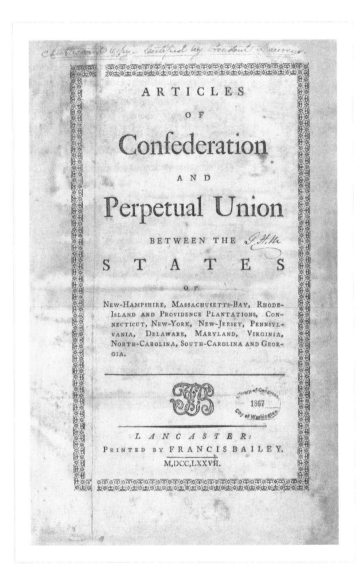

ARTICLES

OF

Confederation

AND

Perpetual Union

BETWEEN THE

STATES

OF

NEW-HAMPSHIRE, MASSACHUSETTS-BAY, RHODE-
ISLAND AND PROVIDENCE PLANTATIONS, CON-
NECTICUT, NEW-YORK, NEW-JERSEY, PENNSYL-
VANIA, DELAWARE, MARYLAND, VIRGINIA,
NORTH-CAROLINA, SOUTH-CAROLINA AND GEOR-
GIA.

LANCASTER:
PRINTED BY FRANCIS BAILEY.
M,DCC,LXXVII.

Francis Bailey

denomination." At the time, the term "sentimentalist" referred to those who believed in the beauty of nature, the inherent worth of human beings and the goodness of God.[8] According to Swedenborg, when the Bible is rightly understood these essential doctrines shine forth from every page. Swedenborg called it the "heavenly doctrine of the New Jerusalem." Johnny Appleseed called it, simply, "Good news, right fresh from heaven."[9]

Among those in attendance at Glen's lecture were Hester Barclay, Francis Bailey, and a man named John Forrester Young, who was studying to be a lawyer. All three became convinced that James Glen had come as a torchbearer of truth. Glen sailed on to his sugar plantation in South America, where, following Swedenborg's ideas, he freed his slaves; Barclay, Bailey, and Young remained in Philadelphia, where they formed a reading group to continue their study of Swedenborg's teachings. The group, which met in the home of Francis Bailey (the official printer for the Continental Congress) was the first Swedenborgian reading group in America. Also included in the circle was Maria Barclay, Hester's niece.

In 1789, John Forrester Young (now an accomplished lawyer) moved his law practice to Greensburg, Pennsylvania,

John Forrester Young

just thirty miles east of Pittsburgh. Greensburg was growing rapidly as an industrial center, immigrants were arriving in huge waves, and lawyers were needed to help settle land claims. Young also helped clients in Philadelphia purchase and sell land expeditiously.

At the same time, the Northwest Territories had recently been opened, and Pittsburgh was booming with trade possibilities. Its geographical position on the confluence of three rivers made it an ideal location for a shipbuilding industry, especially flatboats to take the settlers down the Ohio River and into the newly opened lands. Pittsburgh would have been a convenient place for young Johnny Appleseed to find work, or at least to harvest apple seeds from cider mills. According to Frank O. Chapman:

> John quickly found work in the ship yards building rafts and keel boats for pioneers hastening down the Ohio to find homes in the wilderness. . . General Harris was in command of the fort at Pittsburgh, and owned a large farm on which there was an apple orchard. This orchard especially interested John, and because of his previous experience with trees, General Harris hired him to care for the orchard.[10]

While Johnny was finding employment in Pittsburgh, John Young was gaining recognition in Greensburg. Known as a brilliant and fair-minded attorney with a profound respect for all people and all religions, Young would eventually be appointed "President Judge of our Courts," presiding over five western Pennsylvania counties.[11]

Maria Barclay

In 1794 John Forrester Young married Maria Barclay, one of the original members of the Sweden-borgian reading circle in Philadelphia. Residing now in Greensburg, they continued to be devoted adherents of the new doctrines, and were always eager to share their faith with others.[12]

Meanwhile, back in General Harris's apple orchard (this may have been General *O'Hara*—not *Harris*),[13] Johnny had been distinguishing himself as a hard worker, a dependable person, and a young man of excellent character. Noticing this, it is believed that General Harris (or O'Hara) began to send him on important errands, one of which was a thirty-mile trip to Greensburg with a letter for Judge Young. In addition to the letter from the general, Johnny also carried with him a letter of introduction, allowing the general to formally present the young man to the judge without being physically present.

Johnny not only delivered the letter but also remained to learn about Swedenborgian beliefs. Bright, enthusiastic, and open-minded, Johnny was ready to embrace a theology that showed how God's goodness was manifested not only in the Bible, but also in all of creation. In Swedenborg's theology, Johnny found a faith that could match the love in his heart. And in Judge John Young, who was twelve years his senior, Johnny Appleseed found an able mentor. As Arthur Humphrey puts it:

> Young was renowned for his gentle nature and his charity to strangers, which he often dispensed without verification of need. As a judge he was greatly admired. In difficult cases, he was noted for a tendency to err on the side of leniency. The John Young revealed in Westmoreland County histories was a person whose strong beliefs, shaped by his religion and revealed in his personal and professional life, must certainly have made an enormous impression on John Chapman. A better mentor to Johnny Appleseed there could not have been.[14]

An Extraordinary Missionary

It didn't take long for Johnny Appleseed to start spreading the good news. From home to home he went, armed not only with apple seeds, but also with the seeds of heavenly truth that he found in Swedenborg's writings. As mentioned earlier, Johnny would routinely introduce his readings from Swedenborg by telling people, "I've got good news, right fresh from heaven." And then, if they were interested, he would proceed to read to them. To reinforce his efforts, he divided Swedenborg's books up into chapters, carefully cutting the string that had bound the pages together, leaving sections for the settlers to read on their own. On his next visit he would collect the chapters that he had left with them, leave a new chapter behind, and head on to the next cabin, where he would repeat the process. In this way, he became a one-man circulating library.[15]

Word of his remarkable missionary work spread quickly and even crossed the ocean. In 1817, the Manchester Society for Printing, Publishing and Circulating the Writings of Emanuel Swedenborg, located in England, heard about what was happening. In response, they issued a statement about Johnny's efforts to promote what they called the Church of the New Jerusalem or the New Church:

> There is in the western country a very extraordinary missionary of the New Jerusalem. A man has appeared who seems to be almost independent of corporal wants and sufferings. He goes barefooted, can sleep anywhere, in house or out of house, and live upon the coarsest and most scanty fare. He has actually thawed the ice with his bare feet.
>
> He procures what books he can of the New Church, travels into the remote settlements, and lends them wherever he can find readers, and sometimes divides a book into two or three parts for more extensive distribution and usefulness.
>
> This man for years past has been in the employment of bringing into cultivation, in numberless places in the wilderness, small patches (two or three acres) of ground, and then sowing apple seeds and rearing nurseries.

And then comes this arresting statement:

> The profits of the whole are intended for the purpose
> of enabling him to print all the writings of Emanuel
> Swedenborg, and distribute them through the western
> settlements of the United States.[16]

For most people, this is surprising news. It shines a new light on the story of Johnny Appleseed. He certainly played a vital role in providing seedlings for the early settlers who needed apple trees to survive, and thrive, on the *physical* frontier; but that was not his primary goal. His deeper mission was to share with them the life-giving truths that he found in Swedenborg's writings— truths that would help them survive, and thrive, on the *spiritual* frontier.

Truly, Johnny Appleseed was "an extraordinary missionary of the New Jerusalem."

Books for Land

Was it too good to be true? Perhaps it was all made up. Was it just a fictitious story about a nameless man in America who could thaw ice with his bare feet—another American "tall tale"?

In order to investigate the matter further, a committee was formed with the task of making a full report on this man. Five years later, at the Fifth General Conference of the New Jerusalem, which met in Philadelphia in 1822, a complete report was given. This time there was no mention of tall tales about thawing

ice with bare feet. And this time the extraordinary missionary had a name. He was referred to as "Mr. John Chapman":

> One very extraordinary missionary continued to exert, for
> the spread of divine truth, his modest and humble efforts,
> which would put the most zealous member to blush. We now
> allude to Mr. John Chapman, from whom we are in the habit
> of hearing frequently. His temporal employment consists in
> preceding the settlements, and sowing nurseries of fruit trees,

which he avows to be pursued for the chief purpose of giving him an opportunity of spreading the doctrines throughout the western country.

The report then launches into the highest adulation, describing him as a true hero in the cause of spreading the truths of the New Church:

> In his progress which neither heat nor cold, neither swamps
> nor mountains are permitted to arrest, he carries on his back
> all the New Church publications he can procure, and distrib-
> utes them whenever opportunity is afforded. So great is his
> zeal that he does not hesitate to divide his volumes into parts,
> and, by repeated calls, enable the readers to peruse the whole
> in succession. Having no family, and inured to hardships of
> every kind, his operations are unceasing . . . What shall be the
> reward for such an individual, where as we are told in Holy
> Writ, "They that turn many to righteousness shall shine as the
> stars forever"?[17]

The report seemed conclusive. He was a real person dedicated to what he believed to be a sacred mission. But his extensive missionary activities, including the willingness to share his books so generously, often left Johnny without supplies.

In order to restock, he turned to the organized New Church with a plan to barter land for books—a clear indication of what was most important to Johnny. In a letter written by Daniel Thunn and sent to Margaret Bailey (one of Francis Bailey's daughters), we learn that Johnny had offered to give the church

160 acres of land in exchange for Swedenborgian books. William Schlatter, a prominent New Churchman living in Philadelphia, received a similar offer from Johnny. Writing back to Johnny, Schlatter praised him for his earnest desire "to promote the cause of truth," but said that it was not in his power to "barter books for land." He does, however, refer Johnny to some friends in Cincinnati "who have lately published some of Emanuel Swedenborg's works and might find it possible to exchange some for land." And he concluded his letter by generously offering to send Johnny some books at his own expense.[18]

Undaunted, Johnny looked elsewhere to secure the books he needed. He found a willing supplier in the Rev. Richard Goe, a New Church minister in Wheeling, sixty miles south of Pittsburgh. Reverend Goe writes: "I have sent some books to Mr. Chapman. . . . He travels about in Ohio and has much to do with apple trees; I am told he is a singular man but *greatly in love with the New Church doctrines* and takes great pains in disseminating them."[19]

While Johnny's letters have not survived, a great deal of correspondence from this time period has been preserved, all pointing convincingly to Johnny's ardent desire to promulgate what Swedenborg called the "heavenly doctrine of the New Jerusalem." In fact, Johnny was so enthusiastic about Swedenborg's writings that he was instrumental in forming Swedenborg reading groups in twelve Ohio counties, many of whom organized themselves into church communities.[20]

One of two petitions for the ordination of Silas Ensign, signed by John Chapman
(see page 2, facing). Transcriptions of both petitions appear in appendix D.

Francis Cornwall

Samuel Holmes

Thomas Pyeatte

Jacob Pyeatte

Robert Pyeatte

William Tingley

James Nelson

Wm Hoy

David Kilm

James Kerr

James Arbuckle

David Wilson

Jacob Crow

James Whiteed

John Chapman

In one case, Johnny even took it upon himself to see to it that a Methodist minister, who had recently become a "receiver" of Swedenborg's writings, could be quickly ordained as a New Church minister. Not aware of ecclesiastical red tape, Johnny wrote to William Schlatter in Philadelphia to see about the ordination of the Methodist minister, whose name was Silas Ensign.

Mr. Schlatter wrote back a polite reply: "In reply to your request to have our friend Silas Ensign licensed, I beg leave to point out the regular mode of application which no doubt your society of readers will cheerfully comply with. . . . It is all important to have some regular order in those matters." The "regular order" that Schlatter is referring to is the need for a petition signed by Johnny and the other members of his reading group. Schlatter told him how to go about doing this: "Have a meeting . . . draw up a recommendation . . . forward it to me . . . and your request will be granted," said Schlatter.[21]

Today, the original petition sits securely in a locked vault in the archives of the Swedenborg Library in Bryn Athyn, Pennsylvania. There are thirty-three names on the petition. The last name on the list, written in his distinctive copperplate script, is "John Chapman."[22]

The Man behind the Myths

The Upanishads, which contain the essence of Hindu religion, teach that our essential core is "our deep driving desire." Swedenborg, who had not read the Hindu scriptures, came to the same conclusion. "Love is our life,"[23] he said, or as Vaishali, a modern interpreter of Swedenborg's teachings, says, "You are what you love."[24]

What did Johnny Appleseed love above all things? On one level it might be said that he loved God and his neighbor above all things, thereby fulfilling the two great commandments. But he also loved planting apple trees and making sure that the frontier people were well supplied, even if they couldn't afford it. He loved peace, refusing to take sides in the brutalities that took place among the American Indians and the pioneer settlers—preferring instead to be a mediator. He loved nature, he loved animals, and he loved children. He loved a hot potato, well-salted, on a cold evening, in front of a warm fire. And he loved to tell stories—tall ones, too—just to amuse and entertain. All those things are part of who Johnny Appleseed was.

But he was also, as the minister from Wheeling tells us, "greatly in love with the New Church doctrines." Swedenborg's teachings constituted the core of Johnny's faith, and as nothing else is more deeply seated in a human being than one's faith, it can also be said that it constituted the core of Johnny Appleseed. Knowing this can shed new light on the popular misconceptions that have surrounded Johnny's name for so long.[25]

Let's consider three:

MYTH #1: PANTHEISM

> "Johnny believed that God's life was in everything.
> Therefore, he wouldn't hurt a fly or kill a mosquito."

The universe is a wonderful manifestation of God. But there is a huge difference between asserting that God is *in* everything, and saying that God *is* everything. If Johnny Appleseed were a true pantheist—that is, a person who believes that everything is God—the story about him protecting mosquitoes from the fire would be believable. From a pantheistic point of view, to injure or kill anything, even a mosquito, is to injure or kill God.

Mystics in every religion confess that "the whole world is full of God." In the Bhagavad Gita, for example, Krishna says to Arjuna, "The wise learn to meditate on Me, seeing Me everywhere in everything" (verse 7:19). And Jesus says, "Inasmuch as you did it to one of the least of these My brethren, you did it to Me" (Matthew 25:40).

According to Swedenborg, it is quite true that God is in everything, but this does not mean that everything is God. Here's how Swedenborg explains it:

> We acknowledge that everything in the universe, great and small, has been created by God. That is why the universe and absolutely everything in it is called "the work of Jehovah's hands" . . . This means that the universe, being an image of God [is] therefore full of God . . . While the created universe is not God, it is from God; and since it is from God, his image is in it like the image of a person in a mirror.[26]

Conclusion: Johnny certainly believed that God's life was in everything. But that does not mean that he refused to swat a fly or kill a mosquito. Swedenborg encourages us to worship the Creator and care for the creation—not to worship the creation.

Johnny was not a pantheist, believing that everything is God; he was a Swedenborgian, believing that God is in everything.

MYTH #2: POLYGAMY

*"Johnny believed that if he kept himself sexually pure
in this life, he would be rewarded with two wives in the next life."*

Although Johnny never gave a reason for remaining single, novelists have written beautifully about his loss of a beloved on earth. In *The Quest of John Chapman* by Newell Dwight Hillis, a Romeo-Juliet scenario stands in the way of Johnny marrying his beloved Dorothy, who eventually dies of a broken heart. Johnny never marries, awaiting their reunion in heaven.[27] In *Johnny Appleseed: The Romance of the Sower,* Eleanor Atkinson describes Johnny as having made a covenant with God to provide apple trees for settlers traveling west. This prevents him from marrying his one true love, who, like Dorothy, also dies when very young. Johnny spends the rest of his life single, but is certain that he and his beloved (this time her name is Betty) will be together forever in the next world.[28]

Both stories are works of fiction, but like all great literature, they may be closer to the truth than the stories that arose to fill the vacuum. Swedenborg is very clear that when people are truly in love, their marriage will continue in heaven. God does not separate what he joins together. Even Westley, in the movie *The Princess Bride,* says to his beloved Buttercup, "Death cannot stop true love."

According to Swedenborg, and as many people deeply sense, true love *does* last forever, and there *is* marriage in heaven. Moreover, a married couple in heaven, because of their unity of minds and souls, is called "one angel." Here's how Swedenborg explains it:

> In heaven a married pair is not referred to as two angels but as one. This is the meaning of the Lord's statement that they are no longer two but are one flesh.[29]

> People whose marriages during bodily life were happy because they genuinely loved their spouse have happy marriages in the next world, too. Their happiness carries over from one life into the next, where it becomes a oneness of minds, which holds heaven within it.[30]

> I looked back and forth between the [angel] husband and the wife, and I noticed a kind of oneness of their souls in their faces. I said, "You two are one!" The man answered, "We are one. Her life is in me and mine in her. We are two bodies, but one soul."[31]

And what does Swedenborg say about polygamy?

> The love of polygamy is divided among a number of objects; and a love that is divided is not a love of marriage.[32]

> Angels say that taking more than one wife is absolutely contrary to the divine design . . . the moment that they think about marriage with more than one, they are estranged from their inner blessedness and heavenly happiness.[33]

Conclusion: While little is known about Johnny's reasons for remaining single, we can rule out the idea that he was waiting for a "reward" of two wives in heaven—an unfortunate rumor that was started by a novel written in 1858.[34] Johnny certainly believed that there was marriage in heaven, and must have looked forward to it, but he was not a polygamist; he was a Swedenborgian who knew that true love with one partner can be eternal. He also knew that if he didn't marry on earth, he would find his soulmate in heaven.

MYTH #3: ASCETICISM

"Johnny believed that living without earthly possessions and practicing self-denial would secure him 'snug quarters' in heaven. Therefore, he refused to wear shoes, dressed in rags, and slept outside—all of this out of religious conviction."[35]

As we mentioned earlier, it was not unusual for people to go barefoot for the better part of the year on the American frontier. Johnny may have chosen to go barefoot simply because it was more comfortable, not because he objected to earthly possessions. He did wear ragged clothing, but not because of any religious belief. He just wasn't that into fashion. And he slept outside because he loved to be close to the world that God created, not because he was into self-denial. By all reports, he seems to have been exquisitely happy with the bare essentials: "A few apple-seeds, a few sprouts, a few old books to read, and to him life was full of happiness."[36]

Swedenborg teaches that deliberate abstinence from the basic pleasures of life can lead to a sad, morose existence rather than a happy one. Even worse, these life-denying practices can lead to judgmental attitudes and a sense of superiority—conditions that can suffocate spiritual growth. In brief, Swedenborg encourages people to enjoy their lives, including the vast range of natural delights that God has created for our use and enjoyment. In regard to the idea of "denial," we should by all means deny the selfish demands of the ego, but not the simple pleasures of life.

Swedenborg also cautions about going to the opposite extreme. While he does not condemn the drinking of intoxicating beverages,[37] he does acknowledge that drunkenness can produce beast-like behavior.[38] While he openly champions the importance of sexuality, he is clear that it most properly takes place within marriage. And while he heartily recommends that we enjoy ourselves thoroughly with all the "creature comforts" provided for humanity, he urges his readers to subordinate these "lower loves" to the higher loves of God and the neighbor. Here's how he explains it:

> We may note that it is all right to acquire wealth and accumulate any amount of assets, as long as it is not done by fraud or evil devices. It is all right to eat and drink with elegances, as long as we do not invest our lives in such things. It is all right to be housed as graciously as befits one's station, to chat with others like ourselves, to go to games, to consult about worldly affairs. There is no need to walk around looking pious with a sad, tearful face and a bowed head. We can be happy and cheerful. There is no need to give to the poor except as the

spirit moves us. In short, we can live to all appearances just like worldly people. This is no obstacle to our acceptance into heaven as long as we keep God appropriately in mind and act honestly and fairly toward our neighbors.[39]

Swedenborg adds that this applies also to people who believe they can attain a heavenly reward through pious meditation and withdrawal from the world:

> I have talked after death with some people who during their earthly lives had renounced the world and devoted themselves to a virtually solitary life, wanting to make time for devout meditation by withdrawing their thoughts from worldly matters. They believed that this was the way to follow the path to heaven. In the other life, though, they are gloomy in spirit. They avoid others who are not like themselves and they resent the fact that they are not allotted more happiness than others. They believe they deserve it and do not care about other people, and they avoid the responsibilities of thoughtful behavior that are the means to union with heaven.[40]

For Swedenborg, the way to heaven and heavenly happiness is through a life of useful service—apart from any thought of honor or reward. It is simply a matter of serving others from love. Here's how he puts it:

> The only way we can be formed for heaven is through the world. That is the ultimate goal by which every affection must be defined. Unless affection manifests itself or flows into action, which happens in sizeable communities, it is stifled, ultimately to the point that we no longer focus on our neighbor, but only on ourselves. We can see from this that the life

of thoughtfulness toward our neighbor—behaving fairly and uprightly in all our deeds and in all our responsibilities—leads to heaven, but not a life of piety apart from this active life. . . . Angelic life consists of worthwhile, thoughtful actions, actions that are useful to others . . . *all the happiness angels have is found in service, derives from service, and is proportional to service.* (emphasis added)[41]

Conclusion: It is true that Johnny limited his diet, chose not to engage in war, lived simply, and enjoyed times of solitude, but he did not withdraw from the world. In fact, as a Swedenborgian, he knew that a person's greatest happiness is in living a useful life. Johnny was not an ascetic who believed in renouncing the world; he was a Swedenborgian who believed in fully enjoying the world—especially through service to others.

Unlike the popular folk heroes Davy Crockett, Daniel Boone, and Buffalo Bill, Johnny Appleseed was not a fighting man—at least not physically. He carried no gun, and fought neither man nor beast. Unlike the legendary Paul Bunyan, Johnny will not be remembered for the trees he chopped down, but rather for the seedlings he carefully raised up. As we enter a time when cooperating with others becomes more important than overpowering them, when planting trees becomes more important than paving parking lots, and when improving the planet becomes more important than stripping it, the message of

Johnny Appleseed—and the good news that he disseminated—will take on increasing importance.

In a *New York Times* editorial written in 1951, Johnny is remembered as a true American hero—a person worth emulating, even today:

> The men of his day who sought and gained wealth, power and prestige are long forgotten. Still remembered, as fresh as Ohio apple blossoms, is the simple man who took no care for the morrow as he walked through early American history and brushed close to people's hearts. Perhaps it was because, after all, wealth and power and prestige may not be so hard to achieve; many a man gets them. Johnny Appleseed aimed at something much tougher: to leave the world a more neighborly place than he found it.[42]

John Chapman passed away in 1845 at the age of seventy, in the vicinity of Fort Wayne, Indiana. The exact place of his death has been disputed, but what is not disputable is the beautiful inscription on the marker above his gravesite: "He lived for others."

Swedenborg had a similar message:

> A person is not born to live for oneself alone, but for others.[43]

Frequently Asked Questions about
Johnny Appleseed

Q: *Was Johnny Appleseed a real person?*

A: Yes and no. There was a real person named John Chapman who later became known as "Johnny Appleseed." But over time many stories arose about "Johnny Appleseed" that were more in the realm of legend than reality. So, yes, he was a real person. But many of the legends about him are not real.

Q: *If his real name was John Chapman, how did he get the name "Johnny Appleseed"?*

A: He spent most of his life planting apple trees, which he grew from seed. He even asked children to save their apple seeds for him. As people became accustomed to seeing him with his apple seeds and seedlings, they naturally started to call him "Appleseed John" or "Johnny Appleseed." He even signed some documents as "John Chapman, better known as Johnny Appleseed."

Q: *Where was Johnny Appleseed born?*

A: For a long time, nobody knew. Some people said he was born in Pennsylvania, while others said he was born in Maryland, West

Virginia, or Ohio. Finally, when his official birth record was found, it was settled. He was born in Leominster, Massachusetts, on September 26, 1774.

Q: I heard that one of Johnny's parents was an American Indian. Is that true?

A: It's not true. Johnny's parents, Nathaniel and Elizabeth Chapman, came from a long line of English ancestors. On his father's side, Johnny's ancestors came to America from England in 1639 and settled in Ipswich, Massachusetts. On his mother's side, Johnny's ancestors came to America from England in 1644 and settled in Woburn, Massachusetts. Interestingly, his mother's ancestors arrived on a ship called the *Planter*.

Q: Did Johnny have brothers and sisters?

A: Yes, he did. His sister, Elizabeth (named after her mother), was four years older than Johnny. When Johnny was almost two, and his sister nearly six, their mother gave birth to a third child, a baby boy. Three weeks later their mother died; and two weeks after that the little baby died as well. Four years later, Johnny's father remarried and had ten children. So Johnny had one sister, a brother who died, four half-brothers and six half-sisters.

Q: Where did Johnny Appleseed grow up?

A: Until he was six years old he lived in Leominster, Massachusetts. Then, after his father married a second time, the family moved to Longmeadow, Massachusetts. It was there that Johnny learned to read and write in a beautiful copperplate script. Some say he later attended Harvard College, but officials at Harvard have no record of Johnny ever attending.

Q: Why did Johnny move to the frontier?

A: Longmeadow was on the Connecticut Path, a well-traveled trail that stretched from Boston, Massachusetts, to Albany, New York. Many of the people on the trail were heading west to acquire land, start businesses, and raise families. It was an exciting time, and Johnny probably caught the wave of excitement as wagon trains passed through his town. And so, in 1797, Johnny and his younger brother, Nathaniel, decided to go west. Johnny was twenty-three at the time, and Nathaniel was seventeen.

Q: What route did Johnny take?

A: This question is still under investigation. Some think he took a northern route, traveling through the upper part of Pennsylvania and across New York, heading toward an uncle's cabin in Olean, New York. Others think he traveled down through central Pennsylvania along rivers and over mountain trails. Some people picture him walking along the Pennsylvania Trail, today called the Old Lincoln Highway, which extends from Philadelphia to Pittsburgh. We do know, however, that he first settled along the Allegheny River in western Pennsylvania.

Q: When did Johnny begin his tree-planting business?

A: He could have started as early as 1798. By 1801, he had already started tree nurseries in two Pennsylvania counties and three Ohio counties.

Q: How widespread was Johnny's tree-planting business?

A: When he died in 1845, at the age of seventy, he had planted trees in three states—Pennsylvania, Ohio, and Indiana. It is said that he planted over one hundred thousand square miles of trees, but this is an exaggeration. That would amount to all the land in Pennsylvania and Ohio put together, and a good bit of Indiana as well—64 million acres! While it would have been impossible for him to plant that many trees, he still was quite successful. By the time he died, he had owned over 1,200 acres of land during his lifetime and planted nurseries in nineteen counties across three states.

Q: Is it true that Johnny Appleseed wouldn't hurt a fly or kill a mosquito?

A: Stories like these, which were very popular in Johnny's day, are still repeated today as if they really happened. It is true that Johnny had great respect for nature, and did his best to cooperate with the environment. But stories about his refusal to swat flies or kill mosquitoes are most likely part of the legend that sprang up around him and are probably not true.

Q: Is it true that Johnny never wore shoes and could melt ice with his bare feet?

A: Not true. Like most people in those early pioneer days, Johnny preferred to go barefoot for most of the year. It was easier and cheaper. Also, shoes in those days were not all that comfortable. So he may have gone barefoot even when it started to get cold. But the stories about him walking for long distances in the snow without shoes, or thawing ice with his bare feet, are probably legends. He was tough, and accustomed to a rugged outdoor existence—but he was sensible too.

Q: Did Johnny wear a cooking pot on his head?

A: This is another one of the delightful stories that surround the name of Johnny Appleseed. It is very possible that when Johnny came to town he amused the children by putting his cooking pot on his head sideways—like wearing your baseball cap backwards. Some say that it was a publicity stunt to draw attention to his business. Others say that he wore the pot on his head to protect the religious tracts that he carried with him. But if you put a pot on your head and try to walk around with it, you will soon discover that it is very difficult to do, especially because the pot will keep sliding off your head.

Q: Did Johnny ever get married?

A: As far as we know, Johnny never married.

Q: Did Johnny refuse to marry for religious reasons?

A: Yes and no. Johnny was a Swedenborgian who believed that when the souls of people are united, their union cannot end with death. So, if the woman he was in love with died before they had a chance to be married, he may have believed that their souls were still united. This would be a "religious reason" for not marrying anyone else. But Johnny was not against marriage, nor did he believe that you could attain a higher level of spirituality by choosing not to marry. While this is taught in some religions, this would not have been Johnny's belief.

Q: Can you say a few words about Johnny's religion?

A: Johnny Appleseed was a "Swedenborgian." Just as Lutherans, Calvinists, and Methodists follow the teachings of Martin Luther, John Calvin, and John Wesley, Swedenborgians have a high regard for the teachings of Emanuel Swedenborg, an eighteenth-century scientist and revelator. Swedenborg taught many things about heaven, angels, and how to lead a good life on earth—basically, by

believing in God and keeping the Ten Commandments. He was a
devout Christian, but astonished the world by saying you do not
need to be a Christian to go to heaven. Basically, Swedenborgianism
is about love, wisdom, and useful service—a message that probably
matched the love in Johnny's heart. No wonder Johnny called it
"Good news right fresh from heaven."

Q: So, what can we learn about the story of Johnny Apple-seed that can help us today?

A: That's a good question. In order to answer it, I have asked various
people, "What does the Johnny Appleseed story mean to you?" The
answers are always different, even as every person is different. But
there are common themes. For example, one person was impressed
with how insightful Johnny was, how he was thinking ahead and
planning for the future. Another person said, "For me, Johnny is
a wonderful example of doing what you think is right, all the while
remembering to treat all people with respect and dignity."

Someone else said, "When I think of Johnny Appleseed I just
think about 'spreading'—about spreading what one has to offer,
whatever it is. It's about sharing with others."

A father of a large family said, "It means so much! We sing the
Johnny Appleseed song every night for grace. It's so much fun,
and the harmonies are getting outrageous. It's a sweet song, and it
reminds us that the Lord is good to us."

One thing is certain. The Johnny Appleseed story will continue
to mean different things to different people. To some it will mean
sharing what one has; to others, it might mean being kind to animals
or caring for the environment. Some people will view it as a great
lesson on the importance of living at peace with all people; and some
will see it as a helpful reminder that it is possible to be extremely
happy and contented with only a few things. To some people,

Johnny's story is, above all, an example of how one person can make a big difference, not just in one's own lifetime but also for future generations.

For me, Johnny's story includes all these things, but it also reminds me that priorities are important. Johnny valued truth so much that he was willing to trade land for books, which he would then give to others. While he planted seeds in the American soil, his real desire was to plant truth in the American soul. At least, that's what Johnny's story means to me.

So, what can we learn from the Johnny Appleseed story that can help us today? In the end, this is a question that people will have to decide for themselves. So let's turn the question around. "What does the Johnny Appleseed story mean to *you* and how can it help *you* in your life?"

John Chapman's Ancestry

In both his father's and his mother's line, the ancestry starts with the first person to arrive in what would become the United States. This list is reprinted, with permission, from Robert Price's *Johnny Appleseed: Man and Myth,* courtesy of the Johnny Appleseed Foundation at Urbana University.

Chapman Line

1. Edward Chapman
   b. England, date unknown
   d. Ipswich, Massachusetts, 1678
   Married Mary Symonds

2. John Chapman
   b. Ipswich, Massachusetts, date unknown
   d. Ipswich, Massachusetts, 1677
   Married Rebecca Smith, 1675

3. John Chapman Sr.
   b. Ipswich, Massachusetts, 1676
   d. Tewksbury, Massachusetts, 1739
   Married Elizabeth Davis, 1702

4. John Chapman Jr.
   Baptized, Ipswich, Massachusetts, 1714

d. Tewksbury, Massachusetts, 1760

Married Martha (Perley) Boardman, 1738 or 1739

5. Nathaniel Chapman

    b. Tewksbury, Massachusetts, 1746

    d. Salem (or Lower Salem), Washington County, Ohio,
    1807

    Married (first) Elizabeth Simons (or Simonds) of
    Leominster, Massachusetts, February 8, 1770

    Children: Elizabeth, b. November 18, 1770

    John, b. September 26, 1774 ("Johnny Appleseed")

    Nathaniel, b. June 26, 1776

    Married (second) Lucy Cooley of Longmeadow,
    Massachusetts, July 24, 1780

    Children: Nathaniel, b. December 1781

    Abner, b. July 16, 1783

    Pierly, b. March 6, 1785

    Lucy, b. July 21, 1787

    Patty, b. February 26, 1790

    Persis, b. November 15, 1793

    Mary, b. January 19, 1796

    Jonathan Cooley, b. February 2, 1798

    Davis, b. April 25, 1800

    Sally, b. April 23, 1803

Simonds (Simons) Line

1. William Simonds Sr.

    b. England, date unknown

    d. Woburn, Massachusetts, 1672

    Married Judith (Phippen) Hayward, 1643 or 1644

2. James Simonds

    b. Woburn, Massachusetts, 1658

d. Woburn, Massachusetts, 1717
Married Susanna Blodgett, 1685

3. James Simonds
   b. Woburn, Massachusetts, 1686
   d. Woburn, Massachusetts, 1775
   Married Mary Fowle, 1714

4. James Simons
   b. Woburn, Massachusetts, 1717
   d. Leominster, Massachusetts, date unknown
   Married Anna Lawrence, 1740

5. Elizabeth Simons
   b. Leominster, Massachusetts, 1748 or 1749
   d. Leominster, Massachusetts, 1776
   Married Nathaniel Chapman, February 8, 1770

John Chapman's Nurseries

Traditional as well as documentable nurseries have been listed, but only those for which there is at least one early printed reference. This list is reprinted, with permission, from Robert Price's *Johnny Appleseed: Man and Myth,* courtesy of the Johnny Appleseed Foundation at Urbana University.

Pennsylvania

WARREN COUNTY:

On Big Brokenstraw Creek, "near White's," ca. 1797–1804. (Lansing Wetmore in Warren, PA, Ledger, March 29, 1853: J. S. Schenck and W. S. Rann, eds., *History of Warren County, Pennsylvania,* 1887, 153–4.)

VENANGO COUNTY:

Near Franklin on French Creek, ca. 1798–1804. (Wetmore, loc. cit.; R. I. Curtis in *Ohio Pomological Society Transactions,* 1859, 68–9.)

Ohio

CARROLL COUNTY:

One mile southwest of Carrollton on "the old Ward farm," ca. 1801. (H. J. Eckley, ed., *History of Carroll and Harrison Counties, Ohio,* 1921, I, 15; *Carroll Republican,* February 1887.)

BELMONT COUNTY:

On the headwaters of the Big Stillwater, between Morristown and Freeport, ca. 1801. (J. A. Caldwell, *History of Belmont and Jefferson Counties,* 1880, 191–3.)

JEFFERSON COUNTY:

Near the mouth of George's Run, four miles below Steubenville, opposite Wellsburg, West Virginia, ca. 1801. (Ibid.)

LICKING COUNTY:

On "Scotland Farm, about three miles in a north easterly direction from Newark," ca. 1812. (Isaac Smucker, *Our Pioneers,* 1872, 15.)

COSHOCTON COUNTY:

In New Castle Township, near the blockhouse "at the north-west corner of the Giffin section, on the farm now owned by Daniel McKee," ca. 1807–12. (N. N. Hill, *History of Coshocton County, Ohio,* 1881, 567.)

In Tiverton Township, "near the north line of lot 36, Section 3, a short distance from the Mohican River," ca. 1807–17. (Ibid., 595.)

On "Nursery Island" in the Mohican River, a short distance from the line between Butler Township, Knox County, and Coshocton County, ca. 1807–12. (N. N. Hill, *History of Knox County, Ohio,* (1881, 433.)

KNOX COUNTY:

On the north bank of Owl Creek, in the "Indian Fields" directly west of Center Run, ca. 1807–12. (A. Banning Norton, *A History of Knox County,* Ohio, 1862, xi.)

At Mount Vernon, "on the ground where James W. Forest established his pottery," ca. 1807–12. (Ibid.)

RICHLAND COUNTY:

On the west bank of Rocky Fork, "on the flats, within the present limits of Mansfield, near where once stood the Pittsburgh, Fort Wayne, and Chicago Railway Depot," ca. 1812–20. (H. S. Knapp, *History of the Pioneer and Modern Times of Ashland County*, 1863, 28; A. A. Graham, *History of Richland County, Ohio*, 1880, 269–71; E. Bonar McLaughlin, *Pioneer Directory and Scrap Book . . . of Richland County, Ohio*, 1887, 15.) Between Charles Mills and Mansfield, "on the farm now owned by Mr. Pittinger," no date suggested. (Knapp, loc. cit.)

In Sandusky Township, S. W. Quarter, Section 24, Township 20 N., Range 21 E., ca. 1818. (See "John Chapman's Land Holdings.")

ASHLAND COUNTY:

On the Black Fork, "on the Ruffner quarter section," ca. 1812. (Knapp, 535.)

In Green Township, S. E. Quarter of Section 27, Township 20, Range 16, "near the southeast corner," ca. 1829. (See the John Oliver lease in "John Chapman's Land Holdings.")

On the Black Fork in Green Township, "on the farm now owned by Michael Hogan," N. W. Quarter, Section 20, Township 20 N., Range 16 E, ca. 1815–18. (Knapp, loc. cit.; Mansfield *Ohio Liberal*, August 13, 1873; "John Chapman's Land Holdings.")

On the Black Fork "near Petersburg" (now Mifflinville), no date suggested. (*Ohio Liberal*, August 13, 1873.)

In Orange Township, "where Leidigh's Mill now stands," ca. 1818. (Knapp, loc. cit.)

In Mohican Township, on Jerome Fork, in S. W. Quarter, Section 26, Range 15, Township 31, ca. 1823. ("John Chapman's Land Holdings"; Knapp, 397.)

In Green Township, "on the John Murphy place northeast of the farm owned by the late James Rowland," no date suggested. (Knapp, 308.)

HANCOCK COUNTY:

On the Blanchard River "near the headwaters," ca 1828. (*Putnam County Pioneer Reminiscences*, No. 1, 1878, 60; No. 2, 1887, 45; *History of Defiance County, Ohio*, 1883, 109.)

DEFIANCE COUNTY:

At the mouth of the Tiffin River, about one mile above Defiance, "on lands now owned by Charles Krotz," ca. 1828. (*History of Defiance County*, 1883, 109.)

On the Maumee River "opposite Snaketown" (now Florida), ca. 1829–30. (Ibid.)

ALLEN COUNTY:

Along the Auglaize River, Amanda Township, on land leased of Jacob Harter, 1828. (See "John Chapman's Land Holdings.")

In Amanda Township on Dye Sutherland farm in Section 15, ca. 1828. (*History of Allen County, Ohio*, 1885, 237.)

AUGLAIZE COUNTY:

Along the St. Marys River, south of the city of St. Marys, on land leased of Picket Doute, 1828. (See "John Chapman's Land Holdings.")

In Logan Township on the William Berryman farm in N. E. Quarter, Section 27, ca. 1828. (C. W. Williamson, *History of Western Ohio and Auglaize County*, 1905, 705.)

MERCER COUNTY:

On the St. Marys River below Shanesville (now Rockford) on land leased of William B. Hedges, 1828. (*History of Van Wert and Mercer Counties, Ohio*, 1882, 121–22; "John Chapman's Land Holdings.")

HURON COUNTY:

In New Haven Township, Section 4, "on the lands now owned by George Ganung, on the east side of the marsh," ca. 1825. (*Fire Lands Pioneer,* V, 61–63.)

LOGAN COUNTY:

On Mill Branch, "on the farm now owned by Alonzo and Allen West," ca. 1828 (Joshua Antrim, *History of Champaign and Logan Counties,* 1872, 148–60.)

"Somewhere on Stony Creek," ca. 1828. (Ibid.)

Indiana

ALLEN COUNTY:

Along the north bank of the Maumee River in Milan Township on land purchased in 1834. (See "John Chapman's Land Holdings.")

West of the St. Joseph River in Washington Township, about three miles north of Fort Wayne, ca. 1828 or 1845. (*Ohio Liberal,* August 20, 27, 1873; John W. Dawson, letter in the *Fort Wayne Sentinel,* October 21, 1871.)

JAY COUNTY:

North of the Wabash River in Wabash Township on land purchased in 1836. (See "John Chapman's Land Holdings.")

John Chapman's Land Holdings

This list is reprinted, with permission, from Robert Price's *Johnny Appleseed: Man and Myth,* courtesy of the Johnny Appleseed Foundation at Urbana University.

1797 to 1804. French Creek Township, Venango County, Pennsylvania. "He took up land several times, but would soon find himself without any, by reason of some other person 'jumping' his claim." (J. H. Newton, *History of Venango County, Pennsylvania,* 1879, 595.)

1809. Mount Vernon, Knox County, Ohio. Logs 145 and 147 purchased of Joseph Walker for $50, September 14, 1809. (Knox County Deeds A, 116). Lot 145 sold to Jesse B. Thomas, November 3, 1828, for $30. Entered for record, November 5, 1828. (Ibid., G, 504.)

1814. Washington Township, Richland County, Ohio. N. E. Quarter, Section 1, Township 20, Range 18. 160 acres in Virginia Military District School Lands, value $320. 99-year lease, May 31, 1814, to John Chapman and Jane Cunningham. Contingent expenses $10. One interest payment, 1820, $19.20. Forfeited 1823. (Virginia Military School Land Ledger, Auditor of State, 196.)

1814. Madison Township, Richland County, Ohio, S. E. Quarter, Section 15, Township 21, Range 18. 160 acres, in Virginia Military District School Lands, value $320. 99-year lease, August 22, 1814. Contingent expenses $10. Interest payments, 1822,

$57; 1828, $115; 1829–36, $19.20 yearly; 1837, $7.38 on 70 acres from August 22, 1836; 1838–44, $8.40 yearly. 70 acres forfeited May 28, 1853. (Virginia Military School Land Ledger, 275.) Recorded June 17, 1818. (Richland County Deeds, I, 493.) 90 acres assigned to Alexander Curran and John C. Gilkison, June 1818. (Ibid., 493.) 34 acres assigned to Henry H. Wilcoxen, June 1, 1818. (Ibid., I, 493.) 20 acres assigned to Mathias Day, November 20, 1818. (Ibid., II, 26.)

1815.   Wooster Township, Wayne County, Ohio. N. E. Quarter, Section 21, Township 15, Range 13. 160 acres, in Virginia Military District School Lands, value $320. 99-year lease to Richard Whaley, October 13, 1814; assigned to John Chapman, February 28, 1815, for $100. No further record. (Wayne County Deeds, I, 355.)

1815.   Green Township, Ashland County, Ohio. N. W. Quarter, Section 20, Township 20, Range 16. 160 acres, in Virginia Military District School Lands, value $320. 99-year lease, April 10, 1815. Contingent expenses $10. Recorded, Richland County Deeds, I, 521; Virginia Military School Land Ledger B, 73.)

1818.   Mansfield, Richland County, Ohio, Lot 265, purchased of Henry Wilcoxen for $120, June 1, 1818, recorded August 6, 1818. (Richland County Deeds, I, 523.) Sold to Jesse Edgington, October 30, 1818. (Ibid., I, 614.)

1818.   Sandusky Township, Richland County, Ohio. S. W. Quarter, Section 24, Township 20, Range 20. 160 acres, in Virginia Military District School Lands, value $320. 99-year lease to Moses Modie, June 7, 1815, assigned to William Huff, then to John Chapman, April 27, 1818. No further record. (Richland County Deeds, I, 482.)

1823.   Mohican Township, Ashland County, Ohio. Two and one-half acres in S. W. Quarter, Section 26, Township 21, Range 15, purchased of Alexander Finley, June 25, 1823, for $40. Recorded July 26, 1826. (Wayne County Deeds, IV, 396.) Abandoned.

1825.   Plain Township, Wayne County, Ohio. 14 acres in S. W. Quarter, Section 29, Township 19, Range 14, purchased of Isaac and Minerva Hatch, December 21, 1825, for $60. Recorded July 26, 1826. (Wayne County Deeds, IV, 397.) Sold to John H. Pile, September 8, 1832, for $50. (Ibid., XXXII, 46.)

1826.   Orange Township, Ashland County, Ohio. One-half acre in S. E. Quarter, Section 27, Township 20, Range 16. Leased April 22, 1826, by John Oliver, landlord, to John Chapman, tenant, a piece of ground "where the said John Chapman plants fruit." Term 40 years. Payment 20 apple trees. Recorded August 18, 1829. (Richland County Deeds, VI, 220.)

1828.   Amanda Township, Allen County, Ohio. One-half acre in Section 4, Township 4 South, Range 5 East, "where the said John doth plant an Apple Nursery." Leased of Jacob Harter, __ day of April, 1828. Term 40 years. Payment 40 apple trees at the end of five years. Acknowledged by Jacob Harter, July 16, 1829. Recorded May 17, 1830. (Mercer County Deeds, B, 15.) Payment received, April 13, 1835, and recorded April 14, 1835. (Ibid., C, 188–89.)

1828.   St. Marys Township, Auglaize County, Ohio. One-half acre in Section 10, Township 6, Range 4 East, "where the said John doth plant an Apple Nursery." Leased of Picket Doute, April 6, 1828. Term 40 years. Payment 40 apple trees at the end of five years. Acknowledged by Picket Doute, May 15, 1830. Recorded May 17, 1830. (Ibid., B, 14). Payment received April 2, 1835, and recorded April 2, 1835. (Ibid., C, 177.)

1828.   Dublin Township, Mercer County, Ohio. "A certain enclosed lot or piece of ground lying below the Little Branch, below

Shanesville, between the Little Lane and the River, to John
Chapman for the purpose of sowing apple seeds on, and is to
be cultivated in a nursery for the space of ten years, more or
less. . . ." Leased of William B. Hedges, April 29, 1828. Payment,
1,000 apple trees "to be taken as they average suitable for the
market or transplanting on equal proportion for the space of
ten years . . . on an average of One Hundred Apple Trees per
year . . ." Not recorded. (*History of Van Wert and Mercer Counties,* 1882,
121–22.)

1834.   Milan Township, Allen County, Indiana. Fraction of S. E.
Quarter, Section 28, Township 31 North, Range 14 East.
42.11 acres of canal land, north of the Maumee River at $2.50.
Entered at the Fort Wayne Land Office, April 28, 1834. (Entry
Book, County Auditor; Descriptive Tract Book, Register of
Installments, Wabash and Erie Canal, Auditor of State, 127.)
Final payment, April 28, 1834. (Register of Final Payments,
Wabash and Erie Canal, Auditor of State, 19.)

1834.   Maumee Township, Allen County, Indiana. Fraction of S. E.
Quarter, Section 3, Township 31 North, Range 15 East. 99.03
acres of canal land at $1.50. Entered at the Fort Wayne Land
Office, May 23, 1834. (Entry Book; Descriptive Land Tract
Book.) Final payment, September 21, 1853, in the name of John
F. Swift, purchaser. (Register of Final Payments, 191.)

1834.   Mt. Blanchard Village, Hancock County, Ohio. Lots 51, 52, and
53. Purchased of A. M. Lake, December 24, 1834. Recorded
October 8, 1835. (Hancock County Deeds, I, 830.) Sold to
Michael Shafer, May 20, 1839. (Ibid., III, 118.)

1836.   Maumee Township, Allen County, Indiana. East fraction of S.
E. Quarter, Section 4, Township 31 North, Range 15 East. 18.70
acres at $1.25. Total $23.38. Entered at the Fort Wayne Land
Office, March 10, 1836. (Entry Book.) Application, Receipt, and

Certificate, March 11, 1836; patent March 20, 1837. (General Land Office Records, National Archives, and U. S. Department of the Interior.)

1836. Wabash Township, Jay County, Indiana. S. E. fraction of N. W. Quarter, Section 3, Township 24 North, Range 15 East. 74.04 acres at $1.25. Total $92.55. Entered at the Fort Wayne Land Office, March 11, 1836. (Tract Book, Jay County Recorder's Office, 86.) Application, Receipt, and Certificate, March 11, 1836; patent March 20, 1837 (General Land Office Records, National Archives and U. S. Department of the Interior.)

1838. Eel River Township, Allen County, Indiana. S . E. Quarter of N. W. Quarter, Section 22, Township 32 North, Range 11 East. 40 acres at $1.25. Total $50. Entered at the Fort Wayne Land Office, May 16, 1838. (Entry Book.) Deed Register, State Archives. (Indiana State Library.) Application, Receipt, and Certificate, May 16, 1838. Patent, September 20, 1839. (General Land Office Records, National Archives and U. S. Department of the Interior.)

Petition for the ordination of Silas Ensign from a group in Wooster, Ohio.
Transcription on pages 105–106.

Transcriptions of Original Documents

Advertisement of Swedenborg Lecture

Following is the text of an advertisement for the first public lecture about Emanuel Swedenborg in the United States. The advertisement was placed in three Philadelphia newspapers by the speaker, James Glen. For a reproduction of the original ad, see page 54.

For the Sentimentalists

> A discourse on the Extraordinary Science of Celestial and Terrestrial Connections and Correspondences, recently revived by the late honorable and learned Emanuel Swedenborg, will be delivered by Mr. James Glen, an humble Pupil and Follower of the said Swedenborg's, at half after 7 o'clock, on the Evening of Saturday the 5th of June, 1784, at Bell's Bookstore, near St. Paul's Church, in Third-street, Philadelphia; where Tickets for Admittance may now be had—Price one Quarter Dollar.
>
> This sublime science teaches us from every object in the world of nature, to learn things spiritual and heavenly; it is the most ancient and excellent of all sciences, being that whereby the Holy Scriptures were written; according to which

the earliest of the human race held converse and communication with these blessed Beings.—The knowledge of this
useful science has for many years been lost to this world.—The
honorable Emanuel Swedenborg, the wonderful restorer of
this long lost secret, through the Divine Mercy, had the last
twenty-nine years of his life, through open intercourse [com-
munication] with Spirits and Angels, and was thus taught this
science of Heaven. From his invaluable writings, and conversations with gentlemen who have studied them, the Discourse
hopes to convey some idea and taste of this science of sciences, to the wise and good of every denomination.

Petitions for the Ordination of Silas Ensign

Members of two separate New Church groups in Ohio sent
petitions to the church headquarters in Philadelphia, Pennsylvania, requesting the ordination of Silas Ensign. Original copies of both petitions are preserved in the Swedenborg Library
archives in Bryn Athyn; for a reproduction of the Mansfield
petition, see pages 66–67. The petitions were transcribed by
Page Morahan and Ray Silverman. Possible inaccuracies or
uncertainties about spelling are indicated in brackets.

Petition from the New Church in Mansfield, Ohio

Mansfield, (Ohio) Oct 1st 1822
To the New Jerusalem Society, Phila
To the Honorable Convention of said Society
Respectfully [sheweth];

That your [memorialists] humbly represent to you that we the
undersigned having good confidence and faith of our friend
Silas Ensign as a man of good moral character—a friend to

those who profess religion & has practiced his abilities to
preach the Gospel of Jesus, in this place and the surrounding
neighborhood,

We therefore pray that you as fellow Christians and So-
journers to a throne of grace will take the premises into consideration and grant unto the said Silas Ensign the authority
to preach the Gospel and perform all the duties of a preacher
in the New Jerusalem Church; and your petitioners will ever
pray that God may prosper his labors—is the Prayer of your
Christian Brethren.

James [Rufsee]	Thomas Williams	Robert [Pyeatte]
Robert [Ellrey]	[Triehan L.]	William Tingley
Robert [Croswaite]	James Williams	James [William]
[George Quincy]	[Misha Oleeman]	[William Hay]
Joseph Cairno	John Williams	[Lareh Pilin]
James Wolfe	[Amos] Williams	James Kerr
Elihu Cornwall	Elias Cornwall	James Arbuckle
Solomon Carr	[Tamaris] Cornwall	David Wilson
M. Pollock	Samuel Holmes	[Jacob?] Crum
Benjamin [Tosh]	Thomas [Pyeatte]	Sam [Whitney?]
Joseph Wolham	Jacob [Pyeatte]	John Chapman

Petition from the New Church in Wooster, Ohio

We members and receivers of the Heavenly doctrines of the
Lord's New Church, near Wooster, Wayne County, State of
Ohio, do beg leave to recommend the within named Silas
Ensign to your consideration for the purposes within ex-

pressed and we further represent the said Silas as a man of good moral character and do also request that the said Silas may be ordained a Priest or teaching minister in the Lord's New Church under such restrictions as you in your judgment may think best.

OCTOBER 21, 1822=66*

John S. Tarr	Jeremiah Rogers	Elizabeth Stella
John H. Pile	Sarah C. Tarr	Catherine Tarr
Henry Tarr		

*Note: The number "66" after 1822 indicates the number of years that had passed since 1757, a date noted by Swedenborg as a turning point in the spiritual history of the world.

Acknowledgments

I would like to thank Joanna Hill, executive editor of the Swedenborg Foundation, for suggesting that people need a good book about Johnny Appleseed from a Swedenborgian perspective. I appreciate Joanna's remarkable ability to understand both the core of Swedenborg's message and the needs of modern readers. She provided encouragement, inspiration, and wisdom at every stage of this process.

I am also grateful to Trish Lindsay from the Sower's Chapel in Freeport, Pennsylvania. Living in the midst of Johnny Appleseed country, and being a sixth-generation Swedenborgian herself, she provided me with a wealth of information, not only about Johnny's travels, but especially about his discovery of Swedenborg's writings. She also gave me the key phrase "cultural genius," which we quickly saw applied to both Johnny Appleseed and Steve Jobs. They were both "apple men," aware of people's needs and ahead of their time.

Jean Woods provided valuable information about Judge John Forrester Young—the man who, it is believed, first introduced Johnny Appleseed to the teachings of Emanuel Swedenborg. Not only did she help me sort out complicated family genealogies, but she also shared precious family documents that gave me a better understanding of the life and Swedenborgian beliefs of Judge Young (her great-great-great-grandfather).

Arthur Humphrey led me carefully through the backwoods and mountain trails of western Pennsylvania, helping me get a feel for Johnny's travels, while providing much-appreciated insight about the life and times of the people with whom Johnny associated. Arthur also provided important information about two of his (Arthur's) famous ancestors—Hester Barclay, the earliest female convert to the New Church in America, and her niece Maria Barclay, the wife of Judge John Forrester Young.

Hank Fincken, the noted living history performer who has done over 1,300 one-man shows as Johnny Appleseed, helped me to remember that Johnny loved to have fun. He also reminded me that I needed to pay more attention to the complex relationship between the pioneer settlers and the American Indians.

Surprisingly, help in understanding the relationship between the settlers and the American Indians came from Fredrik Bryntesson, a PhD biologist from Sweden whose great love—ever since childhood—has been the story of the American Indians. Fredrik gave me much-needed advice about how to handle this sensitive subject when it came up in the book.

Joe Besecker, director of the Johnny Appleseed Education Center and Museum in Urbana, Ohio, provided me with unlimited access to the treasure trove of rare materials that he has preserved in the museum. He also helped me to understand that the stories about Johnny, while not always true, are still necessary. "They are part of the fun," said Joe. That insight has meant a lot to me, and has helped tremendously in setting the tone for this book.

Steve Jones, president of Urbana University, and his wife, Judy, generously provided food and shelter during my research trip to Urbana. Beyond being a gracious host, Steve also has a PhD in resources management and a BS in forestry. Consequently, he read the manuscript as a true forester, helping me to tighten up my loose usage of terms like "seedlings," "saplings," "nurseries," and "orchards." He also helped me understand that harvesting trees (not just planting them) can have an important regenerative effect on a whole forest.

William Ellery Jones, founder and director of the Johnny Appleseed Heritage Center (an outdoor theater in Mansfield, Ohio), read through the entire manuscript and offered important editing assistance. He also reminded me that Johnny's story is timeless and touches people in many ways, regardless of their religious background. His book, *Johnny Appleseed: A Voice in the Wilderness,* was especially helpful as an overall guide to my research.

My editor at the Swedenborg Foundation, Morgan Beard, was both encouraging and patient. Her clear understanding of my goal, combined with her wonderful wordsmithing abilities, helped to smooth out the rough edges of the entire manuscript.

Her brilliant insights and perceptive suggestions were always pertinent, and much appreciated.

My daughter, Sasha Silverman, helped me to find accurate phrasing for concepts that were difficult to express, and wisely suggested the pruning of extraneous material. As my daughter, Sasha was especially sensitive to those times when I sounded too "preachy" or slipped into a "moralizing" tone. Without Sasha's perceptive help, I wouldn't have noticed.

Nancy Poes, our illustrator, provided artwork that truly captured the essence of Johnny's spirit, and Karen Connor did an excellent job of arranging Nancy's illustrations. The entire book is blessed by Karen's exceptional design ability and Nancy's delightful artistry.

Finally, I want to thank my wife, Star, whose contributions to this book and to my life are beyond words. She has been with me from the very beginning of this process, reading every revision, always helping me to lead with love. In addition to her remarkable attention to detail, she has helped me to find a tone and a focus that consistently seeks to find the best in people—a true Swedenborgian ideal. Once, when interviewing a couple in the other world, Swedenborg said, "You two are one." The man replied, "We are two bodies but one soul." And then the man added, "She is my heart."

I realize that there are many other people who deserve special mention: Serena Sutton, Melissa Closser, Carroll Odhner, Greg Jackson, Frances Hazard, Wendy Closterman, Sean Lawing, Jack Matthews, Mike West, Marcy Brown, Betsy Coffman,

Page Morahan, Michael Hogan, and Jane Williams-Hogan come to mind. But I know there are many more.

Recently, while driving from my home near Philadelphia to Urbana, Ohio, Arthur Humphrey guided me throughout western Pennsylvania, showing me the many places that Johnny probably visited. The most amazing part of this tour (which took me through forgotten graveyards, into old churches, and over mountain trails) was that Arthur was in Florida, guiding me on Google Earth! Meanwhile, I was walking, hiking, and driving through Pennsylvania, listening to Arthur's directions on my iPhone.

After completing the guided tour, I continued my journey to Ohio, listening to an audio book that I had borrowed from the public library, *Ecological Intelligence* by Daniel Goleman. As I listened to the CD, Goleman said something that arrested my attention. Before forgetting what he said, or losing the idea (and the feeling) that it generated, I quickly made a "voice memo" on my iPhone as my car cruised along Interstate 76. As I close these acknowledgements, I would like to share that memo with you. Here it is, verbatim:

> "Collective Distributed Intelligence." This is what we need in the twenty-first century, says Dan Goleman. I'm thinking of this in terms of the Johnny Appleseed book. I could never have done all of this by myself. All the prior research done by others. The efforts of Joe Besecker at the Johnny Appleseed Museum. Arthur Humphrey. Morgan Beard. My wife, Star. So many people coming together to help me bring to others

the core of Johnny Appleseed. I feel so grateful. "Collective Distributed Intelligence." No one person can do it all. In the coming age, the model is the swarm—a swarm of ants, a swarm of bees, a swarm of human beings, working together, sharing what they know, creating a better world and a brighter tomorrow.

And so, to the whole swarm who gathered to help produce this book, I say, with deepest gratitude, "Thank you!"

——Ray Silverman

Joe Besecker (left) with the author

CHAPTER 1: The Open Road

1. Robert M. Utley and Wilcomb E. Washburn, *Indian Wars* (New York: American Heritage, Inc., 2002), 7–12. See also Bruce A. Robinson, "Genocide of Natives in the Western Hemisphere, starting in 1492," 2008 by the Ontario Consultants on Religious Tolerance. http://www.religioustolerance.org/genocide5.htm (accessed 04/28/2012). Note that the term "American Indian," used throughout this book, may be preferable to the more commonly used term "Native American." See "Why are American Indians and Alaska Natives also referred to as Native Americans?" in the Frequently Asked Questions section of the Bureau of Indian Affairs website (www.bia.gov, accessed May 2012). I am grateful to Dr. A. Fredrik Bryntesson, Hank Fincken, and Chris Hedges for their help in dealing with this sensitive area of American history.

2. For a small fee, individuals who found a parcel of land that they liked could simply apply for a "land-office warrant." As part of the condition to receive a warrant, they would need to hire a surveyor who could accurately describe the land under consideration, including certification that no one else was living there. For a complete description of the process in colonial Pennsylvania, including a copy of an original land grant certificate, see http://www.paland.us/About%20PA%20Land%20Records.htm.

3. Another "great gateway" was Pittsburgh, which we will get to later in the story.

4. The destruction of the buffalo is another sad chapter in North American history. See for example, "Buffalo Slaughter: Greed kills the magnificent prairie beast and changes native life forever." http://www.cbc.ca/history/EPISCONTENTSE1EP10CH2PA2LE.html (accessed 04/28/2012).

5. See, for example, the article by Edward Hoagland, "The Quietly Compelling Legend of America's Gentlest Pioneer," *American Heritage* 31, no. 1 (December 1979). http://www.americanheritage.com/content/johnny-appleseed (accessed 05/02/2012).

6. Walt Disney, *Melody Time,* directed by Clyde Geronomi, et al., (RKO Radio Pictures, 1948). The words and music for the Johnny Appleseed segment, including the song "The Lord is Good to Me" (also known as "The Johnny Appleseed Song"), "The Pioneer Song," and "The Apple Song" are by Kim Gannon (lyrics) and Walter Kent (music). Information provided by Ricky Brigante, Disney consultant at "Inside the Magic," April 17, 2012. The film can be accessed at http://www.youtube.com/watch?v=fVIAIYTJDdw.

7. Johnny's size and height have been variously estimated. Joe Besecker, director of the Johnny Appleseed Museum in Urbana, Ohio, says that the question comes up often. Because no one knows for sure, he likes to say (with a wink), "Johnny is somewhere between five foot five and seven foot seven!" Actually, most reports say that Johnny was about average height, wiry, and very strong. In the *Pioneer Directory and Scrapbook,* compiled by E. Bonar McLaughlin (Richland, Ohio:1887), 22, Johnny is described as "about five feet seven inches tall, straight as an arrow, slim and wiry as a cat."

8. Howard Means, *Johnny Appleseed: The Man, the Myth, the American Story* (New York: Simon and Schuster, 2011), 252.

9. "From these few points you can see how insane people are who think that God can condemn anyone, curse anyone, throw anyone into hell, predestine anyone's soul to eternal death, avenge wrongs, or rage against or punish anyone. . . . In reality, God cannot turn away from us or even look at us with a frown." Emanuel Swedenborg, *True Christianity*, trans. Jonathan S. Rose (West Chester, PA: Swedenborg Foundation, 2006), volume 1, paragraph number 56. Note: All references to Swedenborg's works in this book will refer to paragraph numbers, not page numbers. These paragraph number citations are uniform in all editions.

10. Swedenborg writes, "Because the Lord wants to save everyone, he makes sure that all of us can have our places in heaven if we live well." Emanuel Swedenborg, *Divine Providence*, trans. by George F. Dole (West Chester, PA: Swedenborg Foundation, 2003), paragraph number 254:6.

11. "The laws of this [heavenly] kingdom are eternal truths all based on the law that they should love the Lord above all and their neighbor as themselves. Not only that, but if they wanted to be like the angels, they needed to love their neighbor more than themselves." Emanuel Swedenborg, *Heaven and Hell*, trans. George F. Dole (West Chester, PA: Swedenborg Foundation, 2000), paragraph number 406.

12. Swedenborg writes, "In the spiritual world where we all arrive after death, no one asks what our faith has been or what our beliefs have been, only what our life has been, whether we are one kind of person or another. They know that the quality of our faith and the quality of our beliefs depend on the quality of our life, because life constructs a belief system for itself and constructs a faith for itself." *Divine Providence*, paragraph number 101:3.

13. According to Swedenborg, angels are not superior beings or superhumans. They are real people who once lived on earth and now live

in heaven. While on earth, they freely chose to love God above all things and their neighbor as themselves. This has not changed. As angels, they still continue to love God and serve people. Swedenborg's most comprehensive work, *Secrets of Heaven* (often called by its Latin title, *Arcana Coelestia*) originally published in Latin (London, 1749–56), contains these key teachings about angels: They "hardly even notice evil in another but pay attention instead to everything good and true in the person" (paragraph number 1079:2); they put the best interpretation on what others say and do, excusing them "with all their might" (paragraph number 1085:1); they "think nothing but good and speak nothing but good of others" (paragraph number 1088:2). Swedenborg adds the encouraging thought that we can live *like an angel* while in the world: "If we have good intentions toward our neighbors, though, think only good thoughts about them, and actually do them good when we can, we are associating with angelic spirits and become angels ourselves in the other life" (paragraph number 1680:2). All translations from *Secrets of Heaven* in this volume were done by Lisa Hyatt Cooper. English translations of paragraphs 1–946 were published in *Secrets of Heaven,* vol. 1, trans. Lisa Hyatt Cooper (West Chester, PA: Swedenborg Foundation, 2008) and paragraphs 947–1885 in *Secrets of Heaven,* vol. 2, trans. Lisa Hyatt Cooper (West Chester, PA: Swedenborg Foundation, 2012).

14. Emanuel Swedenborg, *Marriage Love,* paragraph number 7. Originally published in Latin. Amsterdam, 1768. Translations in this volume were done by George F. Dole.

15. Ralph Waldo Emerson, *Representative Men and Other Essays* (London: J. M. Dent and Sons, 1908), 203.

16. According to Joe Besecker, Johnny may have started some of the stories himself. He loved to have fun, and loved to amuse the children with stories. In the "tall tale" tradition of the Midwest, Johnny fully expected people to understand that he was exaggerating—just hav-

ing fun. Over time, however, as the stories were passed along from person to person, they were no longer presented as tall tales, but as actual fact.

CHAPTER 2: The Peel

1. See, for example, Jane Yolen, *Johnny Appleseed: The Legend and the Truth* (New York: HarperCollins, 2008) 2. "Apple blossoms tap the sill/ Welcome baby with a will/Johnny, Johnny Appleseed." Yolen does point out that the birth was actually "on a lovely autumn day."

2. A. Banning Norton, *A History of Knox County Ohio from 1779 to 1862 Inclusive* (Columbus: Richard Nevins, Printer, 1862), 135.

3. Florence E. Wheeler, "John Chapman's Line of Descent from Edward Chapman of Ipswich," *Ohio State Archaeological and Historical Quarterly* 68 (1939): 29–31. The family name was originally Simonds, but later became Simons. In some variations it is Symonds.

4. Robert Price, *Johnny Appleseed: Man and Myth* (Urbana, OH: Urbana University Press, 2001), 10. Originally published by Indiana University Press in 1954.

5. The original letter was first made public by the Johnny Appleseed Memorial Commission, Fort Wayne, Indiana, and published in a mimeographed booklet containing original Johnny Appleseed source material. Robert C. Harris, ed., *Johnny Appleseed Source Book* (Fort Wayne: Public Library of Fort Wayne, 1949), 1. The original version appeared in *The Old Fort News* 9, nos. 1–2 (March–June 1945).

6. From the Longmeadow, Massachusetts, town records: "July 24, 1780, Capt Nath'll Chapman (late of Leominster) and Lucy Cooley of this place were join'd in marriage."

7. Because of extremely scant documentation on this period in Johnny's life, researchers have not been able to come up with anything con-

clusive. However, those who are interested in pursuing the subject in greater depth may appreciate the following e-mail message from Arthur Humphrey (received on 4/23/2012):

> Callender Irvine 1775–1841 was the son of Gen. Wm. Irvine 1741–1804. His father asked him to go to Warren, PA to help settle and develop grant lands he had there. Callender settled specifically at the mouth of the Brokenstraw Creek—where it flows into the Allegheny River.
>
> That this is the precise spot that Chapman and his brother are said to have settled in November 1797 (just before winter set in) seems not to be any coincidence. I personally do not believe that the Chapmans just strolled into town on their own without some sort of job lined up and a place to stay. I firmly believe that if the reports of the two brothers being in Warren and later Franklin, PA are indeed the same Chapmans from Leominster and Longmeadow (there were many Chapmans who settled on lands of the Holland Land Co., in western NY and NW PA) then it was quite probably Callender Irvine who offered them jobs there (clearing land, planting orchards?).

8. Price, *Johnny Appleseed: Man and Myth,* 36.

9. Ibid., 34.

10. Ibid., 32–33.

11. Johnny's older sister had married Nathaniel Rudd and remained in Massachusetts.

12. W. D. Haley, "Johnny Appleseed: A Pioneer Hero," *Harper's New Monthly Magazine* 43 (November 1871): 831.

13. Ophia Smith, *The True Story of Johnny Appleseed* (West Chester, PA: Chrysalis Books, 2007), 28.

14. Michael Pollan, *The Botany of Desire: A Plant's Eye View of the World* (New York: Random House, 2001), 27.

15. Pollan, *The Botany of Desire,* 40. While almost all reports describe Johnny's eyes as being "dark," "black," or "almost black," his leading biographer, Robert Price, says that "he had blue eyes" (Price, 20). Hoagland, perhaps embellishing on Price, adds that Johnny had "piercing blue eyes" (Hoagland, "Quietly Compelling Legend," 3). In this sentence Pollan focuses our attention on what Johnny's eyes *saw,* rather than how they looked: "Johnny Appleseed would show you how to see the divine in nature." As we will see, this insight is crucial in coming to an understanding of the real Johnny Appleseed.

16. Henry Howe, *Historical Collections of Ohio* (Cincinnati, 1847) 2:485–86.

17. Perrin, William Henry, J. H. Battle, and Weston Arthur Goodspeed, *History of Crawford County and Ohio* (Chicago: Baskin and Battey, 1881), 221. http://openlibrary.org/books/OL14699975M/History_of_Crawford_County_and_Ohio (accessed 5/12/2012).

18. Ibid.

19. Howe, *Historical Collections of Ohio,* 485–86.

20. The "Bunyanesque" idea that Johnny planted apple trees in "over a hundred thousand square miles of territory" has been handed down and repeated uncritically by almost all researchers. The first appearance of the statement is by W. D. Haley in his 1871 Harper's article (cited above). The full quote appears toward the end of the article, just before the description of Johnny's last hours and death. It reads: "In the summer of 1847, *when his labors had literally borne fruit over a hundred thousand square miles of territory,* at the close of a warm day, after traveling twenty miles, he entered the house of a settler in Allen County, Indiana, and was as usual warmly welcomed" (836; emphasis added). In reality, "a hundred thousand square miles of territory" would be more than the total square mileage of Ohio and Pennsylvania put together, and a good section of Indiana as well. It would amount to sixty-four million acres! Johnny was a good worker, but surely could not have covered that much territory.

21. Pollan, *The Botany of Desire*, 3.

22. Anne Eliot Crompton, *Johnny's Trail* (New York: Swedenborg Foundation, 1986), 4. The story about Johnny napping while being hotly pursued by Wyandot Indians was originally told by R. I. Curtis in 1859. This was probably the source for Crompton's account. In Curtis's version, however, Johnny eventually falls asleep in the cattails because his pursuers were taking so long to find him. This may have been a "tall tale" that Johnny told to amuse the children, but it may also be based on a true story.

23. Pollan, *The Botany of Desire*, 4. The original incident is recorded by Rosella Rice in 1876, in an article written in *Arthur's Home Magazine*, "Johnny Appleseed." http://www.rosellarice.com/index_files/Page570.htm (accessed 04/28/2012). Miss Rice, who considered herself Johnny Appleseed's first biographer, wrote, "An old uncle of ours, a pioneer in Jefferson county, Ohio, said the first time he ever saw Johnny he was going down the river, 1806, with two canoes lashed together, and well-laden with apple-seeds, which he had obtained at the cider presses of Western Pennsylvania."

24. As told to me by William Ellery Jones, the founder and president of the Johnny Appleseed Heritage Center, Inc., Mansfield, Ohio, April 28, 2012.

25. Joe Besecker, conversation with the author, April 26–27, 2012.

26. Smith, *The True Story of Johnny Appleseed*, 29.

27. Howe, *Historical Collections of Ohio*, 484.

28. Haley, "Johnny Appleseed," 832.

29. Ibid., 831.

30. Ibid.

31. Item from "The Editor's Drawer," *Harper's New Monthly Magazine* 19 (August 1859): 424.

32. Norton, *History of Knox County,* 129.

33. Smith, *The True Story of Johnny Appleseed,* 32.

34. Ibid.

35. "Johnny Appleseed," *Classics Illustrated Junior* (New York: Gilberton Company, 1955), 8.

36. Ibid., 9.

37. Ben Douglass, *A History of Wayne County, Ohio from the Days of the Pioneers and First Settlers to the Present Time* (Indianapolis: Robert Douglas, Publisher, 1878), 198. Douglass's 1879 description of Johnny's respect for all creation erroneously suggests that Johnny is closer to Hindu pantheism than Swedenborgian Christianity: "His convictions relative to the positive sin of visiting pain or death upon any creature was not confined to the higher manifestations of animal life, but everything that had being was to him, in the fact of its life, endowed with so much of the divine essence that to wound or destroy it was to inflict injury upon some atom of Divinity. No Brahmin could be more concerned for the preservation of insect life, and the only occasion on which he destroyed a venomous reptile was a source of long regret, to which he could never refer without a feeling of sorrow."

38. Haley, "Johnny Appleseed," 834.

39. Rosella Rice. http://www.rosellarice.com/index_files/Page570.htm (accessed 04/28/2012). Johnny's care for the animals, including his practice of vegetarianism, suggests Swedenborg's teachings about human nature in its uncorrupted state. Swedenborg writes,

> Regarded in itself, eating meat is a profane custom, since people of the very earliest times never ate the flesh of any animal or bird but only grains (particularly wheat bread), fruit, vegetables, different kinds of milk, and milk products (such as butter). Butchering living creatures and eating the flesh was heinous, in their eyes, and

characteristic of wild beasts. It was only on account of the
menial labor and the functions the animals performed
for them that they captured any. This can be seen from
Genesis 1:29, 30.

   But when time passed and people turned as savage as
wild animals and in fact more savage, for the first time
they started to butcher animals and eat the meat. In view
of the fact that people were like this, the practice was also
tolerated, as it still is today. To the extent that people
follow it in good conscience, it is permissible, because
everything we consider true and consequently allowable
forms our conscience. For this reason, no one these
days is ever condemned for eating meat. (*Secrets of Heaven,*
paragraph no. 1002)

40. This quotation is adapted from *Ishmael* by Dan Quinn (New York:
Bantam, 1992), 239. The main character is being taught the difference between the two kinds of people in the world, the Takers and
the Leavers: "The premise of the Taker story is that *the world belongs to
man. . . . The premise of the Leaver story is that *man belongs to the world."*
(emphasis added)

CHAPTER 3: The Fruit

1.   Price, *Johnny Appleseed: Man and Myth,* 30.

2.   Ibid., 36–37.

3.   Jane Frances Dowd, *Official Roster of the Soldiers of the American Revolution
     Buried in the State of Ohio* (Columbus: F. J. Heer Printing, 1929), 5. State
     of Ohio Library. This information was retrieved at http://archive.
     org/details/officialrosterof1929ohiorich (accessed 04/14/2012).

4.   For many years there was a question about whether or not Johnny's
     father received an honorable discharge. In 2000, convincing
     evidence was found that Captain Nathaniel Chapman was, in fact,
     honorably discharged. See George B. Huff, "Let's Set the Record

Straight," in *Johnny Appleseed: A Voice in the Wilderness,* ed. William Ellery Jones (West Chester, PA: Chrysalis Books, 2000), 96–97.

5. Ibid., 74

6. Price, *Johnny Appleseed: Man and Myth,* 115–16.

7. Perrin, Battle, and Goodspeed, *History of Crawford County,* 19.

8. Ibid., 222.

9. Sam Houston became a senator in February 1846, about eleven months after Johnny passed away. At that time he had also become an honorary citizen of the Cherokee nation, which might explain his admiration and respect for Johnny Appleseed.

10. http://www.chapmanfamilies.org/BIO/appleseed1.pdf (accessed 04/22/2012).

11. See "Religious Offbeat," by Earl L. Douglass, which originally appeared in the *Christian Herald,* August 1961 (Reprinted by the Swedenborg Foundation, New York, 1961), 2–4. Douglass writes, "The word 'offbeat' is a musical term. It is also used of the kind of person who refuses to be bound by the canons of learning and who steps outside, frequently amid ridicule and sometimes under persecution, to make great discoveries. . . . The prophets of Israel were offbeats. . . . Socrates was an offbeat. . . . Columbus was an off beat . . . Galileo defied the scientists of his generation by declaring that the earth revolves about the sun instead of the sun about the earth . . . One of the most amazing offbeats who ever lived was Emanuel Swedenborg. . . . [whose] greatest contribution appears to have been that he put heaven and angels back into men's thought and life."

12. Harris, *Johnny Appleseed Source Book,* 32. For a full list of John Chapman's documented nurseries and land holdings, see appendixes B and C of this book.

13. For a picture of the Dexter City memorial stone, see http://www. roadsideamerica.com/tip/6641.

CHAPTER 4: The Core

1. Frank O. Chapman, "John Chapman (Johnny Appleseed)," a presentation given to the West Virginia Historical Association, Brooke County, April 20, 1967. http://wcbd.hypermart.net/applecrest/johnny1.html (accessed 04/28/2012).

2. Ibid.

3. Smith, *The True Story of Johnny Appleseed*, 20: "Johnny made friends with the Native Americans and spoke their language. They looked upon him with a sort of superstitious awe and considered him a great medicine man. His unusual zeal for serving others led the indigenous tribes to believe him *touched by the Great Spirit. For that reason they allowed him to listen to their council meetings,* and he was therefore sometimes able to avert trouble between the Native Americans and the settlers. Completely free of race consciousness, he understood the viewpoint of both races." (emphasis added)

4. Means, *Johnny Appleseed: The Man, the Myth, the American Story*, 20.

5. Ednah C. Silver, *Sketches of the New Church in America* (Boston: Massachusetts New Church Union, 1920), 9.

6. Hugo Lj. Odhner, "Correspondences in Creation" (unpublished manuscript, 1951), 1–2. Available in the Swedenborg Library, Bryn Athyn, PA.

7. Jack Matthews sums this up beautifully in his article "St. John of the Appletrees." The original article is on file at the Johnny Appleseed Museum in Urbana, Ohio, and reprinted in Matthews's *Memoirs of a Bookman* (Athens: Ohio University Press, 1990), 117–23. "Swedenborg argued that the great panorama of the physical world was only representational, thereby suggestive of another, more marvelous one."

8. Odhner, "Correspondences in Creation," 3.

9. Haley, "Johnny Appleseed," 834. The first reference to the now-famous phrase "Good news right fresh from heaven" appears in W.

D. Haley's 1871 *Harper's* magazine article. The context is worth quoting in full:

> It was his custom, when he had been welcomed to some hospitable log-house after a weary day of journeying, to lie down on the puncheon floor, and after inquiring if his auditors would hear *"some news right fresh from heaven,"* produce his few tattered books, among which would be a New Testament, and read and expound until his uncultivated hearers would catch the spirit and glow of his enthusiasm while they scarcely comprehended his language. A lady who knew him in his later years writes . . . "We can hear him read now, just as we did that summer day when we were busy quilting upstairs, and he lay near the door; his voice rose denunciatory and thrilling—strong and loud as the roar of wind and waves, then soft and soothing as the balmy airs that quivered the morning-glory leaves about his gray beard. His was a strange eloquence at times, and he was undoubtedly a man of genius." (emphasis added)

10. Chapman, "John Chapman (Johnny Appleseed)," 1.

11. John Forrester Young's obituary, which appears in the *Greensburg Sentinel,* October 9, 1840, reports that his appointment as "President Judge" was in 1806. In regard to his respect for all people, regardless of social status or religious preference, Judge Young wrote in his diary, "Amidst the division of tongues, there may be unity of soul [and] the same internal Worship of God." He also writes in his diary that Swedenborg's writings are "the triumph of Christianity." From the private collection of Jean Woods, Mercersburg, Pennsylvania. Viewed on April 30, 2012. Jean Woods is the great-great-great-granddaughter of Judge John Forrester Young and Maria Barclay.

12. This information is from a conversation with Jean Woods on April 30, 2012 (see previous note). Portraits of John and Maria Young, painted by Gilbert Stuart, are available at http://www.wmuseumaa.org/about/getnews.cfm?ID=32.

13. Means, *Johnny Appleseed: The Man, the Myth, the American Story*, 117–18. According to Means this is a possibility, although there is only scant evidence for it. Arthur Humphrey, who originally advanced the idea that this was General James O'Hara, also agrees that we have no conclusive documentation (e-mail communication, April 23, 2012). Here is the pertinent section of Humphrey's e-mail message:

> The other important thing I would like to point out is that I like to err in favor of historical accuracy where I can, and in that, I think it is best to say that no one knows how John Chapman first met John Young, or exactly where. I probably left the impression that I knew the answer to this mystery in the article I wrote in 2006, but in fact I do not. Frank O. Chapman's story of being sent on a business errand for the commander of Fort Pitt (who may or may not have been Gen. James O'Hara) may have some grain of truth to it, but it is not verifiable.

14. Arthur Humphrey, "Greensburg: Johnny Appleseed's Spiritual Nursery," *Westmoreland History Magazine* (Summer 2006): 7. For more information about Judge Young, and his sterling qualities, see George Dallas Albert, *History of Westmoreland County Pennsylvania with Biographical Sketches of Many of Its Pioneers and Prominent Men* (Philadelphia: H. L. Everts, 1882), 303–6, 332–33.

15. Jones, *A Voice in the Wilderness*, 31. Contrary to what is popularly thought, Johnny did not tear pages out of his Bible, nor did he indiscriminately tear apart his Swedenborgian books. Francis Bailey, one of the members of the first Swedenborgian reading circle, and the most prominent printer in America at the time, was printing Swedenborgian books serially in small "octavo" tracts. William Ellery Jones, who owns one of these original tracts, offers this description: "Early Swedenborgian tracts were printed in octavo of six or seven sections, comprising a total of forty-eight or fifty-six pages. The blue-paper covered tracts were stitched together with string in three places and

easily 'separated' into individual sections. Surely, John Chapman was careful not to 'tear' pages from the tracts."

16. Means, *Johnny Appleseed: The Man, the Myth, the American Story*, 192.

17. Price, *Johnny Appleseed: Man and Myth*, 132–33.

18. Ibid., 126–27.

19. Ibid., 125.

20. Hoagland writes, "Between his arrival in central and northern Ohio and the time of his death, Swedenborgian societies sprang up in at least twelve of the counties there, many individuals testifying that it was Chapman, the colporteur of Christian literature, who had first 'planted the seed'" (3). See also Jane Williams-Hogan, "Buckeye Swedenborgians: Impact of a Second Coming Movement in Ohio, 1797–2003" (lecture delivered at Urbana University as a part of the Swedenborg Lecture Series, March 2003). According to Williams-Hogan, by 1843 the New Church in Ohio "had grown from a handful of isolated believers to a vibrant organization with hundreds of members who gathered to worship in forty-eight communities around the state" (33). By 1861 the total membership of the New Church in twenty-seven states was 2,550, but the heaviest concentration of New Church members was in Ohio, with 1,101 members. According to Williams-Hogan, "Swedenborgianism grew and flourished in Ohio when the state was filled with pioneers willing to take risks, willing to innovate and to open themselves to new identities—willing to see and seek heaven as well as earth" (61).

21. Price, *Johnny Appleseed: Man and Myth*, 27.

22. The petition was written by a group in Mansfield, Ohio. A second petition, also in the Swedenborg Library vault, is from another group of "receivers of the Heavenly doctrines of the Lord's New Church, near Wooster Wayne County State of Ohio." In their petition they request that "Silas Ensign may be ordained a Priest or teaching min-

ister within the Lord's New Church under such restrictions as you in your judgment may think best." In due time, both petitions were granted. See appendix D for the full text of both petitions.

23. Emanuel Swedenborg, *Divine Love and Wisdom,* trans. George F. Dole (West Chester, PA: Swedenborg Foundation, 2003), paragraph number 1.

24. Vaishali, *You Are What You Love* (Naples, Florida: Purple Haze Press), x. According to Swedenborg, "If the love in us is for God and our neighbor and consequently for goodness and truth, for what is fair and upright, then no matter how we appear on the outside we are angels as to our spirit, which lives on after death" (*Secrets of Heaven,* paragraph number 6872).

25. Swedenborg, *True Christianity,* paragraph number 601. "Only religion renews and regenerates us. *It is allotted the highest place in the human mind.* Below itself it sees civic concerns that relate to the world. In fact, it rises up through these concerns the way the purest sap rises up through a tree to its very top, and surveys from that height the earthly things that lie below, the way someone looks down from a tower or a high point of land onto the fields below." (emphasis added)

26. Swedenborg, *Divine Love and Wisdom,* paragraph numbers 55, 59.

27. Newell Dwight Hillis, *The Quest of John Chapman* (New York: McMillan, 1904), 26. "Everyone knows that John [Chapman] and Dorothy are made for one another."

28. Eleanor Atkinson, *Johnny Appleseed: The Romance of the Sower* (New York: Harper & Brothers, 1915). The last page of the book (169) describes Johnny's death. His beloved, Betty, has died years before. The last sentence of the page reads, "Johnny was gone to an eternal day with Betty, and to plant orchards in the Garden of God."

29. Swedenborg, *Marriage Love,* paragraph number 50.

30. Swedenborg, *Secrets of Heaven,* paragraph number 2734.

31. Swedenborg, *Marriage Love,* paragraph number 75.

32. Ibid., paragraph number 345.

33. Swedenborg, *Heaven and Hell,* paragraph number 379.

34. Robert Price tells us that this rumor may have been started by James McGaw's novel, *Philip Seymour or Pioneer Life in Richland County Founded on Facts* (Mansfield, Ohio: Herald Steam Press, 1858) 5–6, 22–23, 46, 112. In this fictional work, Johnny is a minor character anticipating "two wives in heaven." See Robert Price, "Johnny Appleseed in American Folklore and Literature," in Jones, *A Voice in the Wilderness,* 14.

35. An obituary for John Chapman, which appeared in the *Fort Wayne Sentinel* on March 22, 1845, perpetuates this mistaken idea: "The deceased . . . denied himself almost [all] the common necessities of life—not so much perhaps for avarice as from his peculiar notions on religious subjects. He was a follower of Swenbog [sic] and devoutly believed that the more he endured in this world, the less he would have to suffer and the greater would be his happiness hereafter—he submitted to every privation with cheerfulness and content, believing that in so doing he was securing snug quarters hereafter." http://www.chapmanfamilies.org/BIO/appleseed1.pdf (accessed 5/2/2012). The title of the article is "Johnny Appleseed." The obituary notice can be found on pages 6–7 of the online article.

36. Norton, *History of Knox County,* 135.

37. "He [Johnny] was regarded as a temperate man, and so he was, but occasionally he would take a dram of spirits to keep himself a little warm, as he said." John W. Dawson, untitled article, *Fort Wayne Sentinel,* October 21 and 23, 1871. See Harris, *Johnny Appleseed Source Book,* 34.

38. Emanuel Swedenborg, *Spiritual Diary: Records and Notes made by Emanuel Swedenborg between 1746 and 1765 from his Experiences in the Spiritual World,* trans. A.W. Acton. (London: Swedenborg Society, 1977), paragraph number 2422. Swedenborg writes that drunkenness is "an enormous sin because a man becomes a brute, and no longer a man . . . and be-

cause he injures his body, and thus precipitates death, besides wasting in luxury what might be of use to many."

39. Swedenborg, *Heaven and Hell,* paragraph number 358.

40. Ibid., paragraph number 360.

41. Ibid., paragraph numbers 360 and 403.

42. Editorial, *New York Times,* April 1, 1951. Quoted by Means, *Johnny Appleseed: The Man, the Myth, the American Story,* 269–70.

43. Swedenborg, *True Christianity,* paragraph number 406.

Sources

Albert, George Dallas. *History of Westmoreland County Pennsylvania with Biographical Sketches of Many of Its Pioneers and Prominent Men.* Philadelphia: H. L. Everts, 1882.

Atkinson, Eleanor. *Johnny Appleseed: The Romance of the Sower.* New York: Harper & Brothers, 1915.

Block, Marguerite Beck. *The New Church in the New World.* New York: Holt, Rinehart and Winston, 1932.

Chapman, Frank O. "John Chapman (Johnny Appleseed)." A presentation given to the West Virginia Historical Association, Brooke County, April 20, 1967.

Crompton, Anne Eliot. *Johnny's Trail.* New York: Swedenborg Foundation, 1986.

Dirlam, Kenneth H. *John Chapman, by Occupation a Gatherer and Planter of Appleseeds.* Mansfield, Ohio, 1954.

Disney, Walt. *Melody Time.* Directed by Clyde Jackson, et al., music by Walter Kent, words and lyrics by Kim Gannon. RKO Radio Pictures, 1948.

Douglass, Ben. *A History of Wayne County, Ohio from the Days of the Pioneers and First Settlers to the Present Time.* Indianapolis: Robert Douglas, Publisher, 1878.

Douglass, Earl L. "Religious Offbeat," *Christian Herald,* August, 1961. Reprinted by the Swedenborg Foundation, New York, 1961.

Dowd, Jane Frances. *Official Roster of the Soldiers of the American Revolution Buried in the State of Ohio.* Columbus: F. J. Heer Printing, 1929.

Emerson, Ralph Waldo. *Representative Men and Other Essays.* London: J. M. Dent and Sons, 1908.

Goleman, Daniel. *Ecological Intelligence.* New York: Broadway Books, 2009.

Haley, W.D. "Johnny Appleseed: A Pioneer Hero." *Harper's New Monthly Magazine* November, 1871.

Harris, Robert C., ed. *Johnny Appleseed Source Book.* Fort Wayne: Public Library of Fort Wayne, 1949. The original version appeared in "The Old Fort News," 9, nos. 1–2, (March–June 1945).

Hillis, Newell Dwight. *The Quest of John Chapman.* New York: McMillan, 1904.

Hoagland, Edward. "The Quietly Compelling Legend of America's Gentlest Pioneer." *American Heritage,* December, 1979.

Howe, Henry. *Historical Collections of Ohio.* 2 vols., Cincinnati, 1847.

Humphrey, Arthur. "Greensburg: Johnny Appleseed's Spiritual Nursery." *Westmoreland History Magazine.* Summer, 2006.

"Johnny Appleseed." *Classics Illustrated* (Junior). Number 515. New York: Gilberton Company, 1966.

Jones, William Ellery, ed. *Johnny Appleseed: A Voice in the Wilderness.* West Chester: Swedenborg Foundation, 2000.

Journal of the Proceedings of the Fifth General Convention of the New Jerusalem. Philadelphia, June 3–5, 1822.

Matthews, Jack. "St. John of the Appletrees." In *Memoirs of a Bookman,* 117–23. Athens: Ohio University Press, 1990.

McGaw, James F. *Philip Seymour; or Pioneer Life in Richland County, Ohio.* Mansfield, Ohio: Herald Steam Press. 1858.

McLaughlin, E. Bonar, compiler. *Pioneer Directory and Scrapbook.* Richland, Ohio: Mansfield Daily News, 1887.

Means, Howard. *Johnny Appleseed: The Man, the Myth, the American Story.* New York: Simon and Schuster, 2011.

Norton, A. Banning. *A History of Knox County Ohio from 1779 to 1862 Inclusive.* Columbus: Richard Nevins, Printer, 1862.

Odhner, Hugo Lj. *Correspondences in Creation.* Unpublished manuscript, 1951. Swedenborg Library, Bryn Athyn, Pennsylvania.

Perrin, William Henry, J. H. Battle, and Weston Arthur Goodspeed. *History of Crawford County and Ohio.* Baskin and Battey, Historical Publishers, 1881.

Pollan, Michael. *The Botany of Desire: A Plant's Eye View of the World.* New York: Random House, 2001.

Price, Robert. *Johnny Appleseed: Man and Myth.* Urbana: Urbana University Press, 2001.

———. "The New England Origins of Johnny Appleseed." *New England Quarterly* 12 (September 1939): 454–69.

Quinn, Daniel. *Ishmael: An Adventure of Mind and Spirit.* New York: Bantam, 1992.

Report of the Society for Printing, Publishing and Circulating the Writings of Emanuel Swedenborg, Manchester, England. January, 14, 1817.

Robinson, Bruce A. "Genocide of Natives in the Western Hemisphere, starting in 1492," Ontario Consultants on Religious Tolerance. Accessed 04/28/2012.

Silver, Ednah C. *Sketches of the New Church in America.* Boston: Massachusetts New Church Union, 1920.

Smith, Ophia. *The True Story of Johnny Appleseed.* West Chester: Chrysalis Books, 2007.

Swedenborg, Emanuel. *Arcana Coelestia.* London: 1749–56. Published in English as *Secrets of Heaven.* Translated by Lisa Hyatt Cooper. 2 vols. (and excerpts from unpublished translations of forthcoming volumes). West Chester, PA: Swedenborg Foundation, 2008–12.

_____. *Delitiae Sapientiae de Amore Conjugiali.* Amsterdam, 1768. Published in English as *Marriage Love.* Translations in this volume by George F. Dole.

_____. *Divine Love and Wisdom.* Translated by George F. Dole. West Chester, PA: Swedenborg Foundation, 2003.

_____. *Divine Providence.* Translated by George F. Dole. West Chester, PA: Swedenborg Foundation, 2003.

_____. *Heaven and Hell.* Translated by George F. Dole. West Chester, PA: Swedenborg Foundation, 2000.

_____. *Spiritual Diary: Records and Notes made by Emanuel Swedenborg between 1746 and 1765 from his Experiences in the Spiritual World.* Translated by A. W. Acton. London: Swedenborg Society, 1977.

_____. *True Christianity.* Translated by Jonathan S. Rose. 2 vols. West Chester, PA: Swedenborg Foundation, 2006–11.

Utley, Robert M., and Wilcomb E. Washburn. *Indian Wars.* New York: American Heritage, Inc., 2002.

Vaishali. *You Are What You Love.* Naples, Florida: Purple Haze Press, 2006.

Wheeler, Florence E. "John Chapman's Line of Descent from Edward Chapman of Ipswich." *Ohio State Archaeological and Historical Quarterly* 48 (1939): 29–31.

Williams-Hogan, Jane. "Buckeye Swedenborgians: Impact of a Second Coming Movement in Ohio, 1797–2003." An unpublished lecture delivered at Urbana University as a part of the Swedenborg Lecture Series, March, 2003.

Yolen, Jane. *Johnny Appleseed: The Legend and the Truth.* New York: HarperCollins, 2008.

Index

Page numbers in *italic* indicate illustrations

Indians. *See* American Indians
IOU issued by John Chapman, 25, *43*
Ipswich, MA, 80
Irvine, Callender and William, 118n7

Jay County, IN, 95, 101
Jefferson County, OH, 92, 120n23
Jesus, 22, 70
Johnny Appleseed. *See* Chapman, John
("Johnny Appleseed")

Knox County, OH, 92, 97

Lake Erie, 28, 40
land grants, 6, 40, 42–43
Leominster, MA, 19, 20, 23, 53, 79–80,
117–18nn6–7
Licking County, OH, 92
Licking Creek, 46
Logan County, OH, 95
Logan Township, OH, 94
Longmeadow, MA, 23–24, 27, 52,
80–81, 117–18nn6–7
"The Lord is Good to Me" (song), 8, 11,
84
love
and Chapman, 71, 83
as a precept of Swedenborg, 14, 68–69,
72, 84
God as pure love, 13, 55
love and marriage, 71–72
love of God and neighbors, 74–75,
115–16nn11,13, 128n24

Madison Township, OH, 97–98
Manchester Society for Printing, Publish-
ing and Circulating the Writings of
Emanuel Swedenborg, 61
Mansfield, OH, 93, 98, 104–106,
127n22
Maumee River, 94, 95, 100
Maumee Township, IN, 100–101

Melody Time (movie), 8–11, 14
Mercer County, OH, 94, 99–100
Mifflinville, OH. *See* Petersburg (now
Mifflinville), OH
Milan Township, IN, 95, 100
Mohican River, 92
Mohican Township, OH, 93, 98–99
Morristown, OH, 92
Mount Vernon, OH, 92, 97
myths about John Chapman, 69–76, 129n35.
See also Chapman, John ("Johnny
Appleseed"), legends and tall tales

Native Americans. *See* American Indians
Newark, OH, 92
New Castle Township, OH, 92
New Church, xi. *See also* Swedenborg,
Emanuel
and Chapman, 60–65, 69
compared to Hinduism, 68–69, 70, 121n37
Fifth General Conference of the New
Jerusalem, 62–64
how the church came to America,
53–55, 57
membership level in 1861, 127n20
ordination of Silas Ensign, *102*,
104–107, 127–28n22
Chapman signs petition, *67*, 68, 106
Swedenborgian societies in Ohio, 65,
104–107, 128–29nn20,22
New Haven Township, OH, 95
New York Times (newspaper) editorial on
Chapman, 77
Northwest Ordinance (1787), 23, 41–43
Northwest Territories, 40, 58
nurseries started by John Chapman,
38–39, 44, 45–46, 48, 61, 63, 89.
See also apple seeds and seedlings; land
holdings of John Chapman
list of nurseries, 46, 81, 91–95
numbers of nurseries owned by, 48,
81–82

O'Hara, James. *See* Harris [or O'Hara], General
Ohio, 18, 29, 38, 42, 77, 80
  Chapman in, 38, 46, 48, 65, 77, 127n20
    land holdings in, 97–100
    nurseries in, 38, 45, 46, 48, 81–82, 91–95
  Daughters of the American Revolution report, 39–41
  Nathaniel Chapman, Jr. in, 27
  Nathaniel Chapman, Sr. in, 41
  population in 1838, 46
  Swedenborgian societies in, 65, 104, 106, 127–28nn20,22
Ohio River, 29, 42, 58
Ohio Valley, 46
Old Lincoln Highway (in Pennsylvania), 81
Orange Township, OH, 93, 99
Owl Creek, 92

pantheist, John Chapman not a, 69–71, 82, 121n37
Pennsylvania, 6, 18, 38, 79, 114n3
  Chapman in, 11, 24–25, 27, 38, 46, 58–59, 81, 120n23
    land holdings in, 97
    nurseries in, 38, 48, 81–82, 91, 119n20
  New Church headquarters in, 68, 104
Pennsylvania Trail, 81
Petersburg (now Mifflinville), OH, 93
Philadelphia, PA, 54, 104
Pittsburgh, PA, 11, 81, 114n3
  booming after opening of Northwest Territories, 58
  Chapman in, 25, 27, 38, 58–59
Plain Township, OH, 99
polygamist, John Chapman not a, 71–73

Richland County, OH, 93, 97–98
rivers and waterways. *See* Allegheny River; Auglaize River; Big Stillwater; Black Fork; Blanchard River; Brokenstraw Creek; Connecticut River; French Creek; George's Run; Jerome Fork; Lake Erie; Licking Creek; Maumee River; Mohican River; Ohio River; Owl Creek; Rocky Fork; St. Joseph River; St. Marys River; Susquehanna River; Tiffin River; Wheeling Creek
Rockford, OH. *See* Shanesville (now Rockford), OH
Rocky Fork, 93

sacred symbolism in the Bible, 54–55
St. Joseph River, 95
St. Marys River, 94
St. Marys Township, OH, 99
Sandusky Township, OH, 93, 98
Schlatter, William, 65, 68
service, importance to Swedenborg, 13–14, 75–76, 77, 84, 115–16n13
Shanesville (now Rockford), OH, 94, 100
signature of John Chapman
  apple tree order with Chapman's signature, *40*
  IOU issued by Chapman, *43*
  on petition for ordination of Silas Ensign, *67*
Simonds (Simons) family lineage, 18–20, 88–89
Simons, Elizabeth (also spelled Simonds). *See* Chapman, Elizabeth Simons (mother)
Snaketown (now Florida), OH, 94
Steubenville, OH, 92
Susquehanna River, 24

Swedenborg, Emanuel, xi, 17. *See also* New
Church
and Chapman as a Swedenborgian,
12–13, 53, 59–60, 62, 64–65,
68–69, 126–27n15
first public lecture about in US, *54,*
54–55, 57, 103–104
symbolism in his writings, 55
teachings of, 12–14, 53–55, 68–69,
83–84
on angels, 13, 115–16n13
on asceticism, 74–76
on basic pleasures of life, 74–75,
129–30n38
fruit trees as living sermons from
God, 55
God is in everything, 70
God's love, 13, 115–16nn9,13
on heaven, 13, 55, 57, 65, 71–72,
73, 83–84, 103, 104, 115–
16nn10–13
human nature in its uncorrupted
state, 121–22n39
importance of religious beliefs,
128n25
living for others, 77
on love, 13, 14, 55, 68–69, 71–72,
74–75, 84, 115–16nn11,13,
128n24
on marriage, 71–72
physical world only representational,
124n7
on polygamy, 72
on salvation, 13, 117n10
on temperance, 74–75, 129–30n38
on useful service, 13–14, 75–76, 77,
84, 117–18n13
and turning point in spiritual history in
1757, 107
Swedenborgian Church. *See* New Church

"tall tales," ix, 18, 19, 76. *See also* Chapman, John ("Johnny Appleseed"),
legends and tall tales
temperance
Swedenborg's teachings about, 74–75,
129–30n38
Chapman as a temperate man, 129n37
Tiffin River, 94
Tiverton Township, OH, 92

Upanishads, 68

Vandorn, E., letter describing John
Chapman, 43–45
vegetarian, John Chapman as a, 121–
22n39
Venango County, PA, 38, 91, 97

Wabash Township, IN, 95, 101
Warren, PA, 24, 25, 118n7
Warren County, PA, 91
Washington Township, IN, 95
Washington Township, OH, 97
Wayne County, OH, 98, 99
Wellsburg, WV, 92
Westmoreland County, PA, 60
Wheeler, Florence, 19
Wheeling, WV, 65, 69
Wheeling Creek, 46
Woburn, MA, 80
Wooster Township, OH, 98
Wyandot Indians, 29, 120n22

Young, John Forrester, 57–60, *58,*
125n11, 126n13